PRAISE FOR
Two Stitches and a Patch

"In this book, Dr. Megli has used a gentle, relatable voice to communicate some difficult tasks in regards to facing death and grief. His stories and illustrations are usable as a grief-recovery tool, counseling handbook, or text for a course on death and grief. This work is valuable and worthy for any counselor, pastor, or person to have in his or her library."

—Christopher K. Cornine, PhD, LPC, NCC, CCMHC, Clinical Director, Diakonos Counseling

We need theologically rich, balanced approaches to death and dying, and Megli certainly offers that. Prepare to be encouraged and prepare to delve deeply into an important subject. Further, be prepared to pass this good work along to other pilgrims on the journey of grief. Thanks for the privilege of sharing this. I really do appreciate your work with this. I think it will be very helpful!"

—Dr. Kenneth J. Parker, Senior Pastor, First Baptist Church, Kearney, Missouri; Professor of Pastoral Ministry and Counseling, Midwestern Baptist Theological Seminary; Author of *Elephants in the Church: What the Bible Says about Fourteen Contemporary Issues*

"*Two Stitches and a Patch* uniquely captures the topic of grief with Terry's own life experiences. Terry does a great job in helping the reader in understanding the Scripture in order to apply it to loss and grief. . . . For all who have experienced or will experience the death of loved ones, this book is a wonderful comfort and a must-read!"

—Debbie Mance, Director of Human Resources,
City Union Mission

"*Two Stitches and a Patch* helps one to understand and process their grief. . . . When a death occurs, it affects our perspective whether we focus on the positive or live in regrets. Grief affects how we relate and connect to others. Or whether we 'stuff' our grief or 'reflect' on their influence and legacy. When a death occurs we are in a time of 'bereavement,' which has the word 'reave' in the middle of the word. That word 'reave' means to 'seize, grasp, lay ahold of, and take something very precious away.' That is what death has done to us; death has taken something very precious away. This book is personal with biblical principles to help understand how Job processed his grief. This book will encourage and give you support in your journey of healing."

—Rev. Roger Megli, Retired Pastor,
Hospice Chaplain, Funeral Home Owner/Director

"[Megli] takes the reader on a worthy journey, hopefully to healing. His tone is very personal, empathetic, and inclusive. He uses good metaphors and good stories, good use of scripture."

—Deborah Loyd, Author of *Your Vocational Credo*, Co-Author of *Dynamic Adventure: A Guide to Starting and Shaping Mission Churches*, Educator, Vocational/Leadership Coach, and Mentor

"I like Terry's book and his counseling on moving from mourning to being revitalized by God's hand of comfort and grace. I like his examples that illustrate his personal growth through the process from grieving to being restored. [He] did a good job on this book. Thanks for letting me read it."

—Rae Lynn Vittorino

"It is well written and I like the short passages with easy places to stop and ponder. (Since I'm a *Peanuts* fan, I liked the 'good grief' mention)."

—Pete Zanias

"I have experienced the loss of multiple people who were deeply connected to me. My general way of dealing with these losses was to do my best to move on and not allow myself to dwell too much in the pain, which would eventually decrease over time. That seemed to me like the successful way to not let it take me over. However, *Two Stiches and a Patch* showed me the value and the gift of experiencing and accepting the grief process in a healthy way, not only for my own benefit but for the benefit of others when consoling them during their grief—whether from a death, a painful relationship, or some other devastating loss. The way Terry tied his own experiences and family stories to explain the concepts and movements were so helpful. This will be a book I'll go back to again and again to contemplate on different aspects of the grief process and their distinct purposes. I'm very glad to have read this book."

—Cindy Bunker

"Death surrounds us. We hear of multiple deaths daily, but they usually don't faze us. Sinister thoughts, emotions, feelings about it do not deal us a gut punch until death strikes down someone we have dearly loved. This book provides comfort and hope to those grieving over the loss of a dear relationship that has been terminated by death. It provides counsel for those that are consoling those suffering under such a great loss. It might even be an encouragement to those approaching their own death. It is packed with wisdom and biblical insight into a topic that is not discussed nearly enough today. I heartily recommend it!"

—Ron Megli

TWO STITCHES AND A PATCH

Two Stitches and a Patch:
Overcoming Grief through the Power of Faith

by Dr. Terry Megli with Robert Lofthouse

© Copyright 2024 Dr. Terry Megli with Robert Lofthouse

ISBN 979-8-88824-322-0

All rights reserved. No part of this publication may be reproduced, stored in a retrieval system, or transmitted in any form or by any means—electronic, mechanical, photocopy, recording, or any other—except for brief quotations in printed reviews, without the prior written permission of the author.

Published by

◤ köehlerbooks™

3705 Shore Drive
Virginia Beach, VA 23455
800-435-4811
www.koehlerbooks.com

Two Stitches and a Patch

Overcoming Grief through the Power of Faith

Dr. Terry Megli
with Robert Lofthouse

VIRGINIA BEACH
CAPE CHARLES

Scripture quotations taken from the (NASB®) New American Standard Bible®, Copyright © 1960, 1971, 1977, 1995, 2020 by The Lockman Foundation. Used by permission. All rights reserved. lockman.org.

TABLE OF CONTENTS

Foreword 1
Introduction 3

Movement I: Reassociating in the Present 11
    Chapter 1: Getting Unstuck 13
    Chapter 2: The Death Talk 19

Movement II: Reinforcing Pain Acceptance 27
    Chapter 3: The Eagle Has Landed 29
    Chapter 4: Divine Prototype 34
    Chapter 5: Cookie Dough 40

Movement III: Reintegrating Safe & Unsafe Emotions 49
    Chapter 6: Don't Hush the Message 51
    Chapter 7: A Grave Interest 56
    Chapter 8: The Lewis Life 60

Movement IV: Reaffirming Past Behavior 69
    Chapter 9: Divine Intervention Physics 71

Movement V: Restoring Your Grip 77
    Chapter 10: Two Scoops of Comfort 79

Movement VI: Recalibrating by Adjusting 85
    Chapter 11: The Final Frontier 87

Movement VII: Revitalizing Our Physical
and Emotional Health 95

    Chapter 12: The Silver Pocket Knife 97

    Chapter 13: The Strawberry Patch Principle 101

    Chapter 14: Commencement 104

Dedication 106
Acknowledgments 107
Bibliography 108

THE SEVEN MOVEMENTS

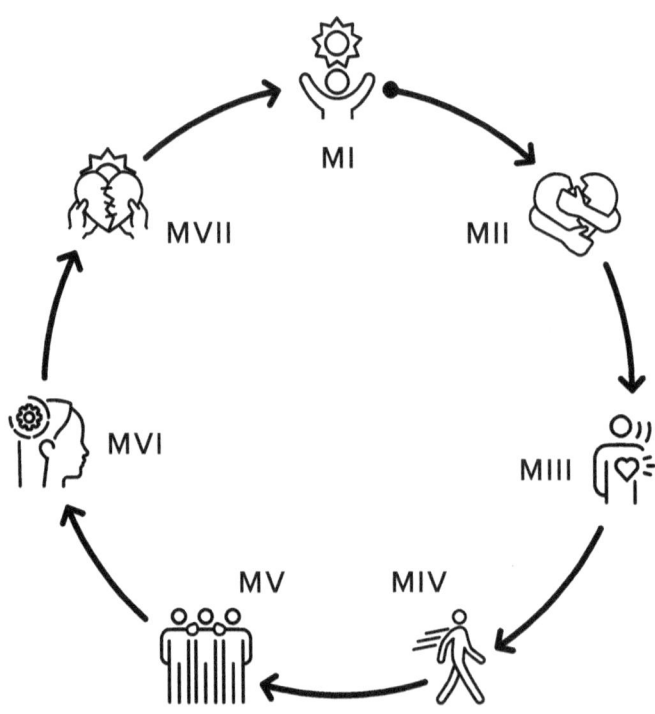

MOVEMENT I: Being present in the moment with self-awareness.

MOVEMENT II: Discovering positive components of a new reality without a loved one.

MOVEMENT III: Expressing emotions while listening to your voice as you reflect on positive memories.

MOVEMENT IV: Acknowledging past behavior as sufficient by focusing on positive movements vs. regrets.

MOVEMENT V: Leaning on supportive relationships that foster godly worth.

MOVEMENT VI: Adjusting to life without the past relationship.

MOVEMENT VII: Achieving a new identity, physical health, emotional health, and spiritual well-being.

FOREWORD

Two Stitches and a Patch is a journey of hope, healing, and health—the kind of journey we must take when life-altering events such as the death of a loved one steer us off course. I may not have experienced trauma as severe as some, but I've learned to watch for how God reveals His love to us in such times and have found that this experience is something we all need to grow through. Enjoying God's love is part of our character development.

In these pages, you will meet my mother, Ruth; my dad, Vernon; my siblings; and my friend Lewis. Each spoke gently into my heart, revealing God's healing hand during my maturation into a man of God. Recovering from grief is a lifelong process and cannot be accomplished in a day.

The title of my book has a dual meaning. Let me explain.

First, in scripture, "two stitches and a patch" refers to how much work a person could accomplish on the Sabbath according to Levitical laws. Ancient Jewish teaching stated that if a garment was snagged or torn on the Sabbath, you were limited to applying only two stitches and a patch of cloth to temporarily hold the garment together. You had to wait for Sunday to arrive before completely repairing the tear. (The Jewish Sabbath was on Saturday, so Sunday was the first day of the week.)

Second, I have fond memories of my mom working the old Singer sewing machine in the guest bedroom. Smoothly rotating, snipping, and readjusting the thread and fabric, she worked wonders, and a beautiful new garment would emerge. She could also stitch anything with leftover patches of cloth, which was often necessary, as five sons and their rough play would have otherwise been expensive.

My brothers and I knew that if something was ripped or torn, Mom would fix it.

Tragedy can rip a hole right through the fabric of your life—but God will fix it. I pray this book will help you feel like He is stitching your ragged, emotional edge into the smooth, silky garment of peace in His presence. It will take time, so be patient.

Jesus arrived to usher in the New Testament era and turned the world upside down. He fed and healed the desperate, grieving, and lame, even on the Sabbath. He gave them hope. I hope He does this with you as He did with me.

I would love to hear from you as you embark on this journey. Feel free to reach out to Terry@MegliLit.com to talk about how God expressed or revealed His love in your life.

I pray to and praise the Lord for His work in walking us all through life's challenges.

Terry

INTRODUCTION

I love books. They open a world of adventure, escape, and virtue.

The Lord revealed to me that the story of what I've gone through needs to be passed down to my children. I've dreamed about writing a book that would encapsulate my heart and allow me to share lessons learned. What kind of book could that be? My children need to know who their dad is and how our wonderful Lord works miracles in our lives regardless of severe setbacks. One of those setbacks is struggling to adapt to a world newly bereft of someone we love—someone who has passed beyond this life and into the next.

Some believe there is life after death. While it is difficult to shake the emotional and physical turmoil of losing someone close to us, the grieving process has a beginning, middle, and end. All three are essential to the human spirit. My purpose in writing these personal stories is to share how I've worked through my grief in the loss of both parents. I also want my children to live well and process whatever grief they encounter in their lives—without holding on to the baggage of regret, remorse, and emptiness. Being capable of nurturing and loving and receiving love is essential.

This book is for all of them. But I realized it is for you, too! I want to share my lessons with anyone experiencing the same void in their heart after losing someone they loved dearly. For the millions of us facing the prospect of death or the loss of a beloved family member or friend, this book offers hope, guidance, and clarity to help us rise out of despair.

Many of us have seen God's handiwork in our lives, but as we journey through life, we encounter trials that stretch our faith and challenge our stamina. Who God is and how He functions in our lives shapes our ability to be resilient and responsive to the study of God.

The experience of losing someone can become a faith-forming moment. Even though grief is normal, it is often a taboo subject and not handled well by most of us—including yours truly. The human spirit needs the emotional release of conversation. We need to be able to talk with someone who cares enough to walk alongside and simply be there for us. I failed to seek this outlet when my parents passed, and I hope you will learn from my mistakes.

We are witnessing a crisis in the Christian community in our failure to practically apply God's grand design in areas like this. This crisis can be averted, and in this book I offer my personal stories so that you too may heal in good order. I will share my hopes, dreams, disappointments, grief, and resolve. Each story is accompanied by scriptural truth and commonsense advice on handling the situation.

Writing this book has been a cathartic process. As I grew in maturity through revisiting the memories of my grief, I learned to console people who came to me for empathy during their grieving time. I hope you find truths in this book to help you walk a similar path to gaining peace of mind. Of course, our situations may differ. We also lose and grieve in many situations that do not involve death. I want to help you accept the reality of your pain while acknowledging that some good can come out of death and other kinds of loss.

And if your painful experience is the death of a loved one, just as the spring season brings new life following the stark cold of winter, you can renew yourself in the belief that you will see your loved one again.

This Is My Story. This Is My Song.

In 1995, when I learned that my dad, Vernon Megli, had passed away, I was stunned.

Although chest pains brought him to a Wichita hospital over Memorial Day, the finality of his presence in that bed did not resonate with me. We would soon learn that his heart bypass surgery of sixteen years earlier had run its course and was no longer effective. So Dad went into his second open-heart surgery at age sixty-nine, and lying in that deathbed for more than a week, he never regained consciousness.

While he was sedated and unconscious, my mother, brothers, and I kept watch, praying and hoping that he would return to normal. The stress of inevitability was overwhelming at times.

My employer, over 100 miles away in Tulsa, was empathetic and supported my decision to stay with my family in Newton, Kansas, north of Wichita, while we waited to see whether Dad was going to survive the surgery. Each day that week, I felt the emotional energy draining out of my mind and body. I was growing weaker. I needed a break. I had to clear my mind, revitalize, rejuvenate, and get my mojo back.

I left the family in Wichita and drove home to Tulsa. The first day back at work felt good. The change of scenery was invigorating, and conversations with coworkers helped to refresh my energy. My decision to take a break from the gravity of the Wesley Medical Center in Wichita felt better with each passing day. I really did believe Dad would wake up and eventually walk out of that place.

When he was healthy, my dad, Vernon, was tough, rugged, and could overcome anything he set his mind to accomplish. He lived through and graduated from the "school of hard knocks." He only had an eighth-grade education in a one-room schoolhouse. But he was smart and brave and developed a strong work ethic.

Growing up in Alberta, Canada, during the Great Depression, when electricity was a luxury, he learned to work hard at a young age. He told stories of the snow being so deep and the visibility so low that his family had to tie a rope between the house's front door and the barn. With that rope to guide them from one to the other to feed the animals, they would not get lost during blizzards—a very real problem for families in the area.

Dad developed enough stamina through these kinds of situations that he qualified for entry into the elite Canadian commando forces during WWII. He became a member of the 1st Canadian Parachute Battalion.

Dad could outstand, outmarch, and outwork anyone! He also solved many complex mechanical problems with his commonsense approach to troubleshooting. He picked up his mechanical know-how by watching and learning from his father, Simon Peter Megli, who was mechanically inclined.

> "I think it's so important for us to hear these stories now, to know what an exceptional time that was for so many and how much they sacrificed to give us the world we have today."
>
> *The Greatest Generation*
> Tom Brokaw

Simon liked steam engines and chain-driven cars and also had a keen interest in electricity. Mind you, Simon began developing his skills in the early years of the twentieth century when cars and electricity were uncommon and certainly not fully evolved in rural central Alberta.

Six months before my dad died, I sought his counsel regarding my career, and he told me, "Terry, someday all these experiences [jobs] will come together in one place. I believe it will happen, and you will then know what you are supposed to do with your life." We did not have many moments like this, but this one was priceless. It came at a time in my young adulthood when I greatly needed his advice.

My hero, my mentor, was gone just as my career and life were taking off. His passing impacted me profoundly, inspiring emotions I had never felt before. Grief settled into my heart and soul. A wound had opened that would take time to heal, but I did not understand this then.

These emotions welled up and hit me hard when I returned to Newton and walked into my parents' home. I kissed and hugged

Mom, then walked downstairs to Dad's office, where my brothers were sorting through his desk papers. They were calm, quietly talking about Dad and looking over his personal items as they prepared for his funeral service. When Ron, my oldest brother, noticed me taking that last step off the stairs, he came over to give me a hug.

I sat on the stairs and sobbed.

The stinging reality of Dad's absence was so painful and shocking that I could not get up. I could have wept all day, but I felt shame in front of my stoic brothers because I was the only one crying. After realizing this and shedding tears for a few minutes, I suppressed those emotions. This suppression put me on a slow path to a state of depression.

My dad modeled toughness, hard work, and putting other people first. When I was young, I never learned how necessary it was to also take care of myself—not just physically but emotionally and spiritually as well. In hindsight, I see that this awareness was profoundly lacking. I, like Dad, would put other people first, ignoring and neglecting my own needs. Those who have been where I was at that point know the feeling.

As we all know, personal problems and feelings we ignore don't just go away.

The more we grow in understanding Jesus, the more we learn how Jesus cares for us and wants us to care for ourselves. Even Jesus faced times when He had to get away from those He was ministering to. Even He needed to rest and regroup by focusing inward. As we seek to put others first, we must appreciate our need for self-care and that we deserve time to rest, relax, and reflect on our emotional and physical requirements.

I did not know about the stages of grief in 1995. The family survived the trauma. Life went on. But that emotional grief would return twenty-two years later in 2017 when my mother died.

I almost did not recognize the feelings oozing back in but soon realized they were the same old, cold, cloudy emotions slowly paralyzing me again. I was still clueless about the grieving phases and had no idea how to handle this trauma. Because I did not understand how people typically respond to grief, I did not feel normal. I was not fully grounded in the teaching of the resurrection and needed more growth to correct that imbalance.

Fast forward to the spring of 2021. I was teaching an adult Sunday school class when I began to sort out these emotions. We were studying the book of Job.

Most are familiar with the phrase "the patience of Job." What does that really mean? The story of Job in the Bible gives us a thorough look at a very wealthy man in ancient times. Because God knew that Job would not lose faith, Satan was allowed to test Job ruthlessly. Job lost his children, 500 yoke of oxen, 500 donkeys, and many servants. He lost all of his wealth, property, and his health. His wife told Job to curse God and die. But Job was resolute in his faith, continued to pray to God for deliverance, and blessed God's name. He never played the role of victim—never asked, "Why me?"

Job is one of my biblical heroes. He showed upright integrity towards God, his family, and his friends. Job's ability to endure the loss of his adult children shows God's hand in his life.

As I studied Job, I discerned "seven movements" of God that are the foundational structure to *Two Stitches and a Patch*. In the following pages, we will look at those seven movements. As we do, I hope you will be able to say, like Job, "My ears have heard of you but now my eyes have seen you" (Job 42:4). When we "see God," we see His handiwork on our hearts.

Before we go any further, we need a road map for the journey to recovery. These seven "rest stops" will give us moments to pause, refresh, reflect, and continue our journey. They can be categorized as the seven "Rs."

We begin in the first movement by "reassociating": being present in the moment with our self-awareness and not disconnecting from our physical and relational needs. The second movement involves "reinforcing" the positive components of a new reality without our loved one. Here we unpack more spiritual awareness of the grieving process. In the third movement, we undertake the process of "reintegrating" by expressing emotions while listening to our voices as we reflect on positive memories and seek the support of others.

The fourth movement is a matter of "reaffirming" our past conduct towards our loved ones as sufficiently loving by focusing on the positive moments versus the deadly pit of regret. The next rest stop in our journey is "restoring" through supportive relationships that give us a sense of true worth and meaning for the next chapter of our lives. The second to last movement involves "recalibrating" by adjusting to life without that lost relationship. Our final destination delves into "revitalizing" our identities, physical health, emotional health, and enhanced spiritual well-being.

That's the patience of Job. Job kept his faith through calamity. He prayed for his friends and remembered his losses. God restored him to more wealth than before and gave him more children and a tenfold increase in livestock. God gave Job renewed purpose.

Two Stitches and a Patch is ultimately about how God steadily repairs our deep wounds with His divine stitchwork. I encourage you to connect the dots of your need for self-care in the ultimate comfort of God, found in the person of Jesus Christ.

> "If you don't pick your future, your future will pick you, and you may not like it."
> Terry Megli, 1989

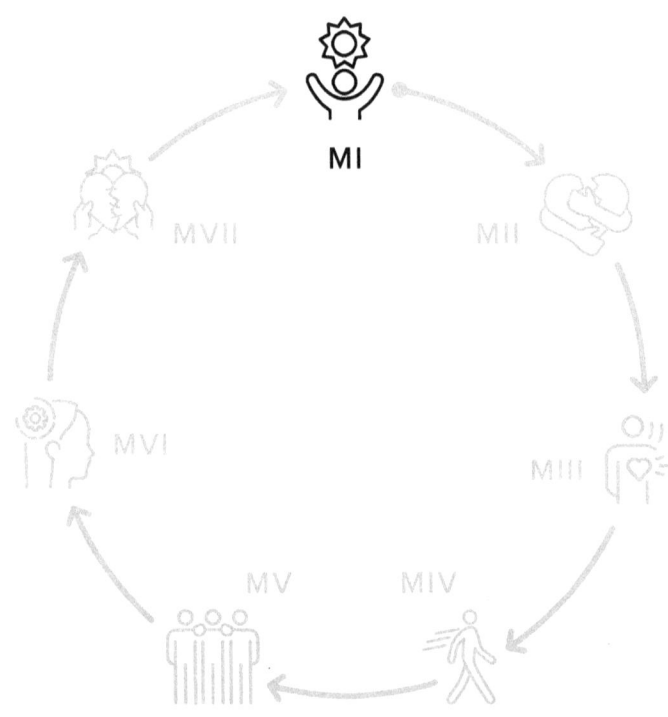

MOVEMENT I: Being present in the moment with self-awareness.

MOVEMENT I

Reassociating in the Present

As we move into our first of seven God movements, we discuss the need to remain present in the moment like Job did, as recounted for us in chapter 2 of the book of Job.

In an act of grief, he stands, tears his robe, shaves his head, and falls on his knees to give back to the Lord.

These feelings roll in like an early-morning fog. When this sensation engulfs our minds, bodies, and soul, current reality goes offline. We feel helpless and maintain only a partial presence with those close to us. This ability to disconnect is how the mind protects itself from the cognitive and emotional threat of pain.

We might no longer engage in everyday activities, be only partially "present," and lie down or sit around a lot. We may wear that "thousand-yard stare" as we drift off into deep thought or no thought at all. The healthy movement at this stage is to reassociate with others and engage in self-care. We must remember that our loved ones are concerned for our welfare.

Job simplifies life into two facts: "The Lord gives and the Lord takes away." Acceptance of these facts is central to this book's message. Let's take the first small step, like Job, to begin to make sense of this movement in our lives. Eventually, our worship of God can help wash the grief stain from the garment of our soul.

CHAPTER 1

Getting Unstuck

"There is an upside of getting stuck, it brings our perspective of God into focus."

The Muck and Mire of Hopelessness

Do you remember scampering outside right after it rained when you were a kid? Playing in the puddles around the yard or floating a boat down the street gutter was great fun! I have a fond memory from when I was six of playing follow-the-leader around our yard with my brother and a neighbor friend.

Our backyard faced a farmer's field past the chain-link fencing. My brother led the way, I was second in line, and my friend Billy brought up the rear. Then came the rain. We were traipsing along the backside of the fence when we started sinking into deep mud. The more we tugged at our feet, the more the mud sucked us back down. Before we knew it, we were stuck up to our knees, the "lifeline" of the fence just out of reach. Our situation seemed hopeless.

Our babysitter watched in wonder as three boys stood there crying, unable to move.

Hearing a commotion outside, Billy's mom opened her back sliding door and had a good laugh, having watched our drama play out on more than one occasion. She knew the boys would be liberated. Sometimes we had to wait for my older brother to come home from high school. He would reach across the fence and pull us out of the muck. It felt like we waited an eternity for that rescue!

When we lose someone close to us, we often sink into a bog of sadness. Not everyone feels regret, but we tend to ponder those negative feelings keeping us "stuck." Feeling stuck in the muck of hopelessness, like us boys in the thick mud, keeps us from imagining a bright future. We might be trapped in this funk for a long time until help comes along.

Let me share another family's experience of hopelessness. They left home during a national economic crisis, hoping to find a better life in a foreign land. Thinking the "grass would be greener," they traveled from Israel to a forbidden place called Moab. This family experienced many of the major traumas we face during an average lifetime.

Moving is always stressful, but in this case, the subsequent death of the husband left the wife alone to manage the household and family affairs. On top of this, both married sons passed away shortly after arriving in Moab, leaving their mother with her two daughters-in-law in an unfamiliar place. Their collective grief, despair, and uncertainty presented compounding challenges.

Wow! What a loss for this family. Three close and interdependent relationships suddenly ceased, and life seemed pointless. Hope for the surviving family members was slim, but God intervened, and the family was eventually restored and redeemed.

What you've just read is the story of Naomi from the book of Ruth.

Perhaps you have felt this kind of sadness and despair. But there is an upside to feeling stuck: it reveals our natural capacity and brings our perspective of God into focus. We learn how He functions in our lives.

Grief Exposes Our Biblical Mindset

Naomi's story takes place during the time of Judges in about 1294 BCE, when there was no king in Israel. Rather than follow God, the people "did what was right in their own eyes" (Judges 17:6).

After Naomi's husband dies, her unchecked grief changes how she views herself, the world around her, and God. Her two sons die sometime after the family arrives in Moab. One daughter-in-law leaves her; one stays. But Naomi is angry about her losses.

Grief distorts Naomi's judgment to the extent that she feels uncomfortable with her identity. Her parents gave her a name that translates to "pleasant." In despair, she changes her name to Mara, meaning "bitter" (Ruth 1:19, 20).

Like many of us who have experienced grief, Naomi/Mara blames God for taking away the men in her family, and she cannot connect with Ruth, the Moabite daughter-in-law who becomes her caregiver. Naomi no longer sees God as "Yahweh," the life giver, but rather "Shaddai," the life destroyer (Ruth 1:20).

> "Yahweh God formed the man from the dust of the ground and breathed into his nostrils the breath of life, and the man became a living being."
>
> Genesis 2:7

God, the sovereign one, grants blessings and life while also pronouncing judgment and taking life. Naomi focuses on the negative qualities of God's sovereignty because she blames him for taking away her happiness. The book of Deuteronomy reinforces God's sovereign right to determine who lives and who dies, including whom He chooses to heal (Deuteronomy 32:39).

Like Naomi, we might be tempted to look beyond God, feeling that all hope is lost, and to refuse the help of others who mean well. Trauma survivors often waffle in their spiritual beliefs as they attempt to make temporal sense of the life-changing event. Overwhelming thoughts of living life without our loved ones can shake our sense of reality.

This dysfunctional thinking rationalizes that the God of the past (when our loved one was alive) is not the God of the present nor the future (now that our loved one is gone). God becomes "uncomfortable" and "unsafe" to us in this moment.

Grief Exposes Unhealthy Thoughts

Near and present death presents a unique predicament for each person. If we have not worked on identifying our feelings and the thoughts behind them during everyday issues, we will struggle here and possibly get stuck in our grief. Grief might demotivate us to do what brings pleasure. Our lack of desire to eat or talk about our feelings becomes the new normal for a while.

This malaise means we have work to do in our healing. Naomi/Mara demonstrates the classic dysfunctional mindset of not feeling worthy of life and pushing away the positive relationships available to her.

The goal of this movement in the grieving process is to strengthen those existing relationships so we can weather the current storm. There are many Naomis around us, adult survivors who struggle with traumatic loss. Some, like Ruth, find hope in a redeemer-kinsman like Boaz, but do not be surprised if your Naomi refuses to connect relationally.

In biblical times, as a point of reference, if a married man died with no son, the redeemer could marry his widow to ensure the continuation of the family line. This practice is most famously depicted in the story of Ruth and Boaz, who were descended from the same lineage. References to this practice are also found in the books of Leviticus (25:47–49, 27:9–25) and Ruth (3:9-13).

I'm not suggesting the continuation of this practice in the literal sense; a redeemer-kinsman isn't relevant in most modern legal systems today. However, the underlying themes of family responsibility, caring for the vulnerable, and seeking justice are still applicable.

The figure of the redeemer-kinsman can also be interpreted symbolically, as a foreshadowing of Jesus Christ, the ultimate redeemer who liberates humanity from the death grip of sin.

Grief Exposes Healthy Connections

Grief is an invisible curtain ripped open by traumatic events to expose the truth, like the Wizard of Oz's booth in the 1939 movie.

In the movie, Dorothy subconsciously sees herself as missing a brain, a heart, and courage and finds her alter ego in the Scarecrow, the Tin Man, and the Lion. The movie metaphorically expresses our inability to appreciate those already in our supportive circle of relationships. Dorothy discovers that when she needs help thinking through life's problems, the encouragement to do the right thing materializes before her eyes because of her foundation in those very relationships. By following her heart, she learns to embrace the connections she previously devalued.

At one time or another, like Dorothy, we all face sudden negative emotions, get overwhelmed by intolerable feelings, and seek to retreat from and separate from supportive relationships. When the grief cord is pulled, eventually we see the healthy, supportive relationships that were there all along.

Our comforters may not know the right words to use, but their love for us is reflected through their presence and willingness to be helpful.

Good Grief! Bad Grief!

When I was younger, I always looked forward to the *Wichita Eagle Beacon* Sunday edition for the full-color insert of comics in the back. I would ask Mom to read them to me every Sunday afternoon before my nap. I still remember her soft voice and her laugh as she read Charles Schulz's *Peanuts*.

Charlie Brown would often say, "Good grief!" Though it comes across as a humorous remark, I believe Charlie was onto something; good and bad grief do exist. Blaming others for the loss of our loved ones is "bad grief." Blaming God is bad theology. Bad grief chooses not to work through the reality of this death and suspends the growth cycle of final acceptance.

Good grief accepts reality and adjusts to a new lifestyle that brings about wholeness and contains peace and positive memory recall of our loved ones.

As an example of positive memories and experiences that connect us to those we've lost, I am a huge military historian, which overlaps with my dad's WWII stories and artifacts. I have pictures of him in uniform and his coveted parachute "jump" ring, awarded for finishing jump school. Holding and looking at his WWII pictures fosters a deeper appreciation for his life. When I do this, the bad thoughts get filtered out, and the good ones are revitalized, enhancing my "good grief" healing.

So, we have a choice. We can choose to remain in our bitterness, focusing on the tragedy, trauma, and troubling effects of this sudden loss. Or we can choose to connect to objects or memories that will strengthen their memory. There is a time for mourning loss, and both paths take lots of energy, but only one restores our souls and heals our pain. Which will it be for you?

CHAPTER 2

The Death Talk

"We learn to accept that life without our loved ones will be a different but acceptable experience."

A sick man turned to his doctor as he was preparing to leave the examination room and said, "Doctor, I am afraid to die. Tell me what lies on the other side."

Very quietly, the doctor said, "I don't know."

"You don't know? You're a Christian man and don't know what's on the other side?"

The doctor was holding the door handle; from the other side came the sound of scratching and whining, and as he opened the door, a dog sprang into the room and leaped on him with an eager show of gladness.

Turning to the patient, the doctor said, "Did you notice my dog? He's never been in this room before. He didn't know what was inside. He knew nothing except that his master was here, and when the door opened, he sprang in without fear. I know little of what is on the other side of death, but I do know one thing. I know my Master is there, and that is enough."

—Based on *Death: What a wonderful way to explain it* (Author Unknown)[1]

---

[1] Coach Muller, "Death...A Wonderful Way to Explain It," *My Good Time Stories* (blog), April 3, 2021, https://mygoodtimestories.com/2021/04/03/death-a-wonderful-way-to-explain-it/.

Do you remember your first driving lesson? I do. My house was just down the street from our new high school facility, which had a massive parking lot for the students and faculty. My dad took my brother and me in Mom's 1972 Chevy Impala with a rigid vinyl top.

In the parking lot, he gave us the "car talk" with the solemnity of handing off the nuclear football briefcase to a fifteen-year-old. Now as a dad, I project the same tone of seriousness to my two boys.

Dad's instruction was explicit: A car is a loaded weapon; it can kill someone. Driving is not a right but a reward for responsibility. If the car does not feel, smell, or look right, stop driving and seek help.

We were blessed to have a dad who took the time to give us these big life lessons so we could grow up to be responsible adults. During my time in ministry, I have met many adults who did not receive that kind of parental coaching to facilitate their growth. Like learning the mindset of driving, many did not learn critical insights from what I call the "death talk."

Consider Jesus your driving coach in the passenger seat.

I am reminded of Jesus's death talks with the disciples. Jesus's last night with His disciples in the upper room is a celebration of Passover, but it is also an opportunity to say goodbye to them and prepare them for His absence. He talks about hard things like suffering, rejection, and being killed. Three times, Jesus predicts His death. Can you imagine the most influential person in your life warning about their impending death multiple times? Jesus is their best friend, their surrogate father, their source of life and meaning, and He is calmly discussing His life coming to a sudden end.

We find the content of this death talk in John's Gospel, chapter 14. Jesus can read His disciples' fear of being left behind without His presence. He does not adopt the serious tone of car talk but instead uses comforting words to give His friends a springboard into the future. He wants them to remember this as a soothing, teachable moment. He speaks with love and compassion, knowing that losing a loved one would be hard for their earthly hearts to handle.

Look at His loving words: "believe," "prepare," "assurance," and "comforter." Jesus seems to be stitching their frayed emotions into the smooth, silky garment of God's comforting presence.

During my middle school years, having personalized, embroidered denim shirts was cool. Trends usually start with one kid, and everyone else runs home and tells their mom to make them one. I was that kid. Our mom was that mom who embroidered names, animals, and bicycles all over our shirts. This is what Jesus did with His closest friends. He stitched hope to their future.

The death talk acknowledges that every human being has a life cycle. Our mom and dad helped me and my brothers understand this. Let's move through the talking points so you can embrace what is written. Buckle up, adjust your mirrors, and push the seat into position for your first driving lesson on death.

Principle #1: Death Is Normal and Part of the Life Cycle

Life will end for everyone. We must all adjust to living a new life of meaning and purpose without a loved one. This termination of life results from the fall of Adam and Eve (Genesis 3). Their consumption of the forbidden fruit encoded the death DNA in all of us.

So, no one will live forever in their current state of physical reality. To believe otherwise is to deny the reality of death.

Principle #2: Some Things Are Worse than Death

My mother reminded us boys of this concept while growing up.

Death for the deceased means there are no adjustments, no lingering pain, and no emotional turmoil to work through. Death ends all our human senses. Alternately, if we lose one or more of our senses or a limb, this might fall under the category of being worse than death in terms of having to make a life adjustment.

Below are other examples of circumstances that may be worse than death:

- Seeing our children suffer an incurable sickness or disease
- Going through physical or emotional abuse
- Experiencing the betrayal of a close friend or loved one
- Suffering the destruction of a lifetime of memories by a house fire
- Enduring the life-altering effects of a tragic auto accident
- Living in a paralyzed body
- Caring for a brain-damaged child

Some people adapt to these life-changing, traumatic events on their own. Some need the help of experts and the comfort of close relationships. You may already have experienced some of these events, so perhaps you can attest to how painful it is to make the necessary adjustments. Ultimately, death is not as traumatic as we might perceive it to be. Survivors living with their loss often confront a more significant challenge.

Principle #3: Life Will Be Different, but It Will Be Okay

Here is an example of this principle: Tom lost his father a year ago but recently has experienced a downward emotional spiral. When his father passed away, no one talked about their grief. Aside from sobbing and tears, grief was suppressed, and talking about Dad was not encouraged. He and his family never discussed an emotional path forward and what life would look like in the coming weeks and months. Tom is unaware that his depression and dysfunctional behavior are connected to the anniversary of his father's passing.

The trauma of realizing we've just lost someone can distort our judgment for a period. Time and distance from that memory can clarify a distorted situation. Accepting the loss or change cycle calms the mind and allows us to adjust and resume normal activities. We learn to accept that life without our loved ones will be a different but acceptable experience. Additionally, working through change often brings a new level of thinking, feeling, and behaving towards others.

Prior to my mom's passing, not knowing what to say to a client with a parent in hospice was a struggle for me as a counselor. Due to that hospice experience, I am now more compassionate and understanding of those going through the same thing.

Framework of the Death Talk

Our emotional responses to traumatic events and the subconscious messages shaping our self-worth control the release of automatic negative thoughts. Healthy death talks will help us rethink the situation by reframing events.

Going back to the book of Ruth, our new understanding of emotional responses to trauma connects the dots in Naomi's story, giving us insight into why she responds to the death of her husband and sons in the way described in Scripture. We want something better for ourselves.

The death talk prepares us mentally and emotionally to walk through the end-of-life stages with our loved ones. Through professionals trained in trauma care, we can filter out harmful messages and distorted understanding of what is happening. Emerging from the fog of grief gives clarity to the experience. It is important to understand that the physical relationship will be exchanged for memories, and the sharp emotional pain will fade. The pain still registers, but it won't be as intense as it was at the outset of our suffering.

Death is the beginning of a short separation. Those who understand this framework of death can be used by God to minister to others in love.

Doula

When my wife gave birth to our oldest son, we were assigned a doula, or birth companion. The doula provided prebirth, delivery, and post birth care to the mother and infant. Knowledgeable in bringing life into the world, she relieved my anxiety.

Death needs a companion as well. An end-of-life death doula assists family members and the person dying, providing companionship while the individual walks through that death door.

One such example was my mother. During her funeral reception, I learned she was a death doula, sitting for hours and comforting many people as they lay on their deathbeds. Hospice was not fully developed in the '70s and '80s, so people relied on friends who could help provide respite. As a nurse, Mom was compassionate and comforted the dying with conversation, praying with or for them and simply holding their hands. She was a rare individual. She knew a lot about death, having lost her mother to kidney disease and her dad to heart failure when she was just twenty-one. This mercy ministry is a high calling within the body of Christ. Those with the gift of "helps" most likely fit within this definition.

The ability to render a helping ministry to those dying has the same value as a birth doula. Both life and death doulas seek to bring the best care, comfort, and love and the presence of Christ in the room when needed.

I trust this new "stitching" brings perspective to your ragged edge of grief. Understanding the basics of death helps us navigate those deep potholes of depression and panic. We, like the disciples, need a word of truth, comfort, and inspiration to keep moving forward with a deeper sense of God's purpose.

For more answers to your questions or more information, hover over this QR code and follow the link to our website.

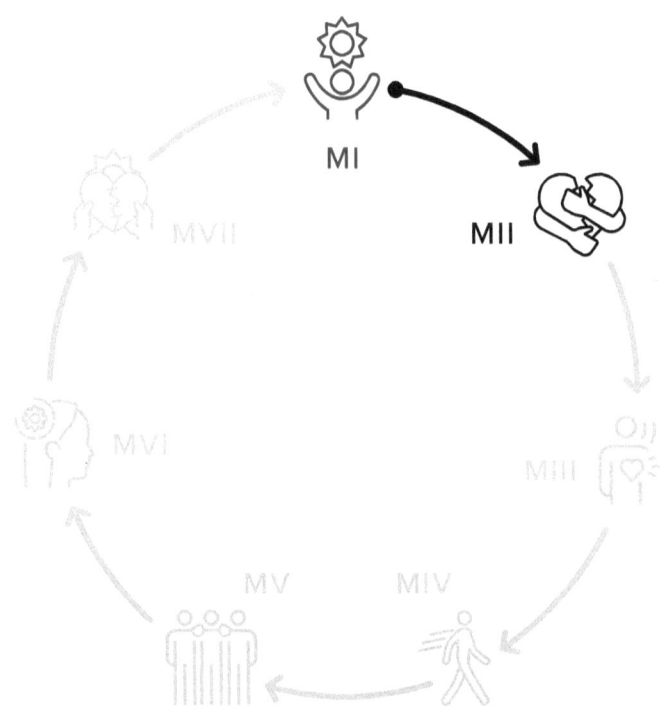

MOVEMENT II: Discovering positive components of a new reality without a loved one.

MOVEMENT II

Reinforcing Pain Acceptance

The second movement in this change process is the ability to reinforce the positive components of a new reality without our loved ones.

Returning to the book of Job, Job initially desires God to take away his pain by ending his life outright. However, God allows pain into our lives to serve a greater purpose down the road. This greater purpose remains a mystery on this side of Heaven, but for the believer, this grieving process will strengthen our love for and faith in the Lord.

Job acknowledges that his strength in himself is not enough; he can only accept the unrelenting pain (Job 6:11–13). He cooperates with this movement and keeps from sliding back into the fog of disconnection from God and others.

Reinforcing is similar to applying super glue to two pieces of a broken whole. The glue is applied to one side, and with the correct pressure and timing, the two pieces become one unit again. Our new, healthy self-awareness must likewise be bonded to our ability to manage this new acceptance. Like with the glue, pressure and time is required. Eventually, a stronger, more resilient mindset develops.

This section explores the divine bonding agent that will instill courage and trust in our Heavenly Father.

CHAPTER 3

The Eagle Has Landed

"If you need a better glimpse of God, I am sure someone can lift you on their shoulders."

I was three years old when my family visited Disneyland in August 1969. The Apollo 11 astronauts had just returned from a successful landing on the moon and were visiting Los Angeles International Airport after a ticker tape parade in New York City. After touchdown, they would be shuttled to President Nixon's California residence via helicopter for a private dinner with their commander in chief.

My parents learned of the imminent landing of Air Force One, so off we went to see the most famous men in America. We left Disneyland and drove to the airport. Slipping under the fence, we snuck in for a closer look, standing right on the tarmac near the private welcoming party. I was lifted onto my brother Roger's shoulders, and he pointed out the astronauts who had walked on the moon. It felt like a miracle had happened for mankind, and I was there to witness it.

Those brave men trained for years, working through their fears to perform flawlessly at great risk to their lives in outer space. Our bodies are not meant to live outside the earth's atmosphere, where we cannot breathe and would float away due to lack of oxygen and gravity. NASA works hard to keep their personnel safe and healthy for long periods of space flight by enclosing them in protective space suits and a space vehicle that can withstand the extreme temperatures.

The dynamics at play here point to another form of physics beyond our understanding of the natural order. NASA assesses candidates' ability to adapt to constant stress and life-threatening challenges during a mission. Not everyone is disciplined enough. Astronauts' training and divine hard-wiring allow them to adapt and remain calm when alarms go off in space. Similarly, the ability to increase our capacities during times of stress resides in our souls. The resilience and motivation to step into a new reality derives from the divine DNA coding God gave us at our conception.

Many who flew on these NASA missions quoted the first chapter of Genesis while orbiting the planet. Like us earthbound humans, astronauts probably contemplate death, and this kind of thinking opens the door to exploring elements beyond our limited understanding. The Bible strategically reveals these mysteries through divine physics, instrumental in the redemption of humanity. When Apollo 11 landed on the moon on July 20, 1969, Edwin "Buzz" Aldrin gave thanks to God through the act of Communion. In the same way, our faith connection links us to a life that extends into eternity and beyond: an afterlife.

The life, death, and resurrection of Christ provide fundamental proof that the natural order extends beyond human control and comprehension. Life is unpredictable, and dynamics outside our human understanding intersect with the divine. The intersection of grief with our usual routines causes a disruption limited by our finite understanding.

The sting of loss goes to our hurt lockers and leaves scars on our souls. The ability to move towards a joyful life after losing a loved one is rooted in the love and comfort of God (2 Corinthians 1:3–4*). Divine intervention inflates our emotional flat tires and keeps us on the road of hope for God's eternal plan. Despite the curse brought about by Adam and Eve's sin, the creative order still opens the door for believers to have an eternal life with Him.

> "³Blessed be the God and Father of our Lord Jesus Christ, the Father of mercies and God of all comfort, ⁴who comforts us in all our affliction so that we will be able to comfort those who are in [a]any affliction with the comfort with which we ourselves are comforted by God."
>
> 2 Corinthians 1:3-4

This Is Our Hope

Our first glimpse of hope is in the biblical appearance of a person with no beginning and no end to his existence, as described in Hebrews chapter 7. Abraham (known as Abram) learns that his nephew Lot and his family have been kidnapped. This ignites the fear of losing someone Abram cares for deeply, so he acts. He raises an army, attacks the captors during the night, and rescues Lot and the other captives.

On his way back from this victory, Abram encounters the king of Salem, known only as Melchizedek, who shares his bread and wine while blessing Abram. Melchizedek is described in Genesis 14:18 as "priest of the Most High." Abram presents part of the plunder from his victory to Melchizedek as a tithe. In his own way, he acknowledges the lordship of this most high priest.

Through God's eternal plan, a preexisting, preincarnate Christ known as Melchizedek passed through the creative-natural-order barrier to intervene in a moment of crisis and subsequently disappeared. His appearance has ripple effects in our understanding of what a miracle is.

Get a Grip

In middle school wrestling, we learned that our starting grip or approach was not the one we would ultimately use to beat our opponents. This is also true of the death grip. To experience joy, peace, and victory over this opponent (death), we must adjust our grip—in other words, how we manage the conflict. In addition, if we do not learn the proper footwork, we will not succeed. These aspects work hand in glove. We need a new working framework of pivots and grips opened to the truth of God's work in us.

I hope you are ready to walk this path with me and adjust your grip on the concept and meaning of death, because your soul demands it. Your soul wants it. Your soul depends on it. Otherwise, rather than gaining a victorious grip on your grief and making life-saving adjustments, you may be stuck in a dysfunctional grip, leading to hopelessness and despair.

The key to unlocking a victorious grip on the death antagonist begins with understanding the core of who Christ is and why He is at the center of our ability to overcome death. This understanding requires unpacking key miracles in the lives of God's people, as described in His Word, the Holy Bible.

For starters, we'll walk through scriptural stories of these miracles to better understand how God intervened and how people responded and then discuss how to position our feet for better leverage while dealing with our own death conflicts.

Back to Space

During Apollo 11's descent to the moon's surface, the lunar module computer detected a serious malfunction in the sequence of tasks required to land safely. Within seconds of the alarm going off, Buzz had to make a critical decision: should he manually take over the landing or allow the computer to sort out what was most vital?

He had a "grip" in understanding this computer technology, how it would intervene and complete the landing. With his training as a fighter pilot, his tendency was to take control, but his faith and confidence in the engineering won out. He left it to the computer to resolve the situation.

We need to master this same kind of grip on the inner workings of divine healing.

> Divine healing is defined as a supernatural act of God that resolves a physical, emotional, or spiritual sickness. It is healing only achieved by God through Jesus and the prayers of His people. Some would simply say it is the answer to a prayer for health or reconciliation.[2]

Healing that worked yesterday works today and will work tomorrow. God will bring divine healing again and again. Just as Buzz Aldrin trusted in the Apollo computer, we must trust in God's promises. God is faithful and reliable and will carry us through the darkest times of our lives.

During humanity's first physical intersection with another planetary object, NASA announced, "The Eagle has landed!" It is now your turn to experience God's landing in your heart. He has a plan for you. If you need a better glimpse of God, I am sure someone can lift you onto their shoulders. This may be an opportunity to seek out a pastor, elder, deacon, or a good church—or you may reach out to me.

Join me as we take this journey.

---

[2] Ashley Hooker, "What Is Divine Healing, and Does It Happen Today," Crosswalk, Salem Web Network, July 15, 2022, https://www.crosswalk.com/faith/spiritual-life/what-is-divine-healing-and-does-it-happen-today.html.

CHAPTER 4

Divine Prototype

"Hold tight to God's unseen hand, and the movements of God become self-evident."

In 1983, I encountered my first computer in our high school lab—an IBM. Computers were a novel concept until my algebra/geometry teacher received funding within the math department. The disk operating system (DOS) required writing math formulas within the line-item commands. Many students did not know we could take the course as a substitute for the math requirement.

My girlfriend's brother, a math whiz, was already tinkering with computers. These first models were bulky, slow, and difficult to comprehend—certainly not user friendly. There were few rules and guidelines. Everyone was making it up as they went along. I struggled to make a D+ in the class; computers were not for me, apparently. Then, in 1988, my girlfriend and soon-to-be bride acquired an Apple IIc computer. This futuristic monitor and keyboard with an interchangeable joystick and "mouse" blew me away! It also had an internal speaker and headphone jack—space-age stuff in my hot little hands over thirty years ago.

At that time, few people sensed that this was where computer technology was headed. The keyboard design laid the foundation for laptop computers with a forward-facing keyboard attached to the frame. We both regret not keeping it, like many things in life that come and go. To me, the Apple IIc was a divine gift sent from God through Steve Jobs. If my first exposure to computers had been to an Apple system, who knows where life would have taken me?

As I write this book on a MacBook Pro laptop computer, it is a far cry from those old DOS days. Who would have guessed back then that the power of a computer mainframe, which once occupied an entire air-conditioned room, could be embedded in a smartphone that fits in your pocket?

A prototype takes an abstract concept and establishes a framework for making it reality. It allows our minds to pivot and embrace creative ideas we'd never imagined. Prototypes are usually scaled-down versions created to validate the efficacy of a new system of thinking. Successful prototypes are then scaled up, and the working system components are perfected for the final, complete unit.

Some systems will be designed within form and function. Some systems will be designed completely outside the box.

God's miracles are like prototypes. They are samples, models, or tested design concepts. These divine prototypes are part of the inner workings of God's divine action physics (DAP) system. This DAP is the operating system that interprets the preprogrammed mind of God, the operating code. The essence of miracles is the how, what, and where they present themselves. This DAP has many elements, including death. Death can be a causal loop that restricts the growth of miracles in our earthly lives.

You may be wondering, *How will this help me in my current funk? How does this relate?* Remember, we seek to bring divine action healing into our lives. When we learn a new grip, it usually starts awkwardly, as with anything new. Just ask a golfer who has been instructed by a golfing coach to change a grip they've used for years. It does not feel natural in any sense. But we adapt, learn, and practice with the new grip, and it soon becomes routine and no longer awkward.

First Grip Lesson: Unlearning a Bad Grip

Melchizedek is the first link in adjusting our new grip on Christ, who ultimately has control, power, and glory over death. Melchizedek mysteriously shows up in Genesis with Abram, and then scripture is silent on this person for hundreds of years. Genesis provides an initial indication of who this king of Salem is: Christ preincarnate. Christ is later identified as the high priest within the order of Melchizedek (Hebrews 5:5–10). "Order" in this context is a system of rules and processes.

This concept of preincarnation means that Christ physically stepped into man's time continuum and appeared to Abram in physical form long before taking on another human embodiment through the virgin birth. King David confirms this in Psalm 110, where he describes adjusting his footwork to understand who Melchizedek is. Here David displays both his historical perspective on life and his righteousness over his opponents.

In Hebrews, the DAP system allows the temporary reversal of God's creative order where a person exists outside of our natural realm of birth and death, enters our timeline for a purpose, then exits. How does Christ beat the system? Through divine physics.

Second Grip Lesson: God's "Stargate Portal"

The order of Melchizedek cannot be traced from physical ancestry; it is based upon the power of an "indestructible life" (Hebrews 7:16).

This preincarnation element opens the possibility of a "divine portal" that allows God to move freely back and forth throughout His creation without disrupting the natural order. The divine physics power motif points to a new grip in understanding. If God could miraculously suspend the natural physical order to allow His preexisting son to preside over Abram's blessing, then He could certainly give His son permanent human flesh through a virgin birth and bring His son back from death. We cannot pick and choose what miracles make sense. Holding tightly to the virgin birth but rejecting the physics of divine dynamics in play with His appearance to Abram is just not possible.

God can do more than we comprehend. In Abram's day, Jesus's time had not yet come, but that is another story. Melchizedek's life will not decay as do human lives. The appearance of Melchizedek ties the red thread of divine physics through the virgin birth and Jesus's death, resurrection, and ascension, eventually leading to our own glorious lives after death.

Third Grip Lesson: Loosing Death's Grip

Lot avoids certain death due to the intervention of Abram and his 318 armed men, who confront an enormous army. God's presence enables Abram to see His ultimate control over life and death. Like Abram, we must acknowledge the reality of heavenly dynamics beyond our earthly comprehension, even in moments of deep despair. Lot likewise learns that his finite life was created with meaning and purpose (Genesis 1:26).

This is true for those of us held hostage by the shadow of death. The roller coaster of emotions tempts us to doubt that our lives have purpose. We most desperately seek these interventions when we are overwhelmed with despair and loss. Our soul endlessly searches for a divine solution. We pray for God to "do something."

So, how do we loosen death's grip? Do we try to avoid thinking about death or our deceased loved one? No; it is impossible, or folly, to deny life's troubles. How then do we release the dark fog death has cast on us? Is bad grief a good thing?

Divine healing can take place in these moments of change. Melchizedek's brief appearance to bless Abram is a clear sign of God's involvement in our lives. God's love may be unseen, but it manifests in those miraculous ways we seek. We do not see the wind, but we see the leaves move and feel the air across our skin.

Take, for instance, a well-grounded "religious" man in the New Testament who has trouble grasping the reality of miracles he does not understand, so he sets up a covert meeting with Jesus at night. This is a pivotal moment for Nicodemus in terms of getting a grip on God's unseen movements. Nicodemus regards Jesus as a great teacher. He has the proper footwork, and Christ helps him readjust his grip, leading to a transformative spiritual birth. This requires a new paradigm, a new way of thinking (John 3).

Did you catch that? To loosen our grip on death, we need to acknowledge the effects of God in our lives like we do the reality of wind. We can only feel and see the consequences, the miracle, and not the thing itself—never God. Embracing Christ's life-changing work on the cross through faith releases the paralyzing grip of death on our hearts and minds.

Practice Session Over: We Are Not in Kansas Anymore

Beginning with the correct grip provides a sense of cognitive control in processing the physics of the divine from our earthbound perspective. The wrong grip will bring about a false sense of control over the idea of death and losing someone.

This may be hard to hear, but divine love is so much deeper than a finite, temporal, human love. That includes the love we share with our parents, children, pets, siblings, and other loved ones. Death separates us from receiving love from our departed loved ones. However, the divine love of God supersedes death; there is no infinite separation between life and death for the believer.

We will be transformed (1 Corinthians 15:52) after that significant life event. The divine physics surrounding Melchizedek is the same that produced the miracle of the resurrection and will facilitate our transition into eternity.

As we have learned, there is no single grip we can use on death. We must constantly adjust our footwork and adapt our grip on reality. Divine action healing is a major comfort because it contains dynamics of love, meaningful connections, purpose, and ultimately "peace that passes all understanding" (Philippians 4:7). Each adjustment opens more opportunities to deepen our understanding of our pain. We must not fight this; rather, we must steer into the power of God's presence to heal our hurt. He will give us hope in the miracle of life after death; this is a fact and not a feeling.

Hold tight to God's unseen hand, and the movements of God become self-evident.

CHAPTER 5

Cookie Dough

"Courage means being a risk-taker in moments
when we feel paralyzed and helpless."

I love eating chocolate chip cookie dough! I have a sweet memory of sneaking spoonfuls of dough from Mom's large yellow bowl in the refrigerator. This kind of behavior usually resulted in a stern scolding if she caught me. She would say, "Cookie dough will make you sick." For my brothers and me, the tasty dough was worth the risk. Flour, sugar, eggs, vanilla, chocolate chips, and butter—as a child, I was captivated by how the ingredients worked together to create a delicious outcome.

Just like cookie dough, God has a way of blending ingredients and transforming reality to captivate us. This blending of supernatural ingredients is called a miracle.

Charlton Heston in Cecile B. DeMille's movie *The Ten Commandments* (1956) also fascinated me growing up. The day before every Palm Sunday, we would tune in to this movie on our black-and-white TV, eventually in color. The parting of the Red Sea is a prime example of the interrelated system of actions and counteractions within our natural world that represents DAP working in the background.

The word "miracle" is defined as a sign or wonder. What do miracles point toward if they are signs? The aroma of baking cookies triggers our taste buds to salivate in anticipation of something tasty. Miracles are like this as well. Something marvelous is happening, and there is more to come. Miracles act as signs of a supernatural encounter with God.

For each of the four definitions below, we will look at a contemporary movie example, then dive into an explanation of each concept. Let's unpack the four key ingredients of DAP.

Transmutation

Do you remember the disabled Marine in the *Avatar* (2009) movie? Jake gains a genetically engineered alien body and possesses it through a technology that accesses his brain. In essence, he experiences transmutation. However, the possession is not permanent at first.

Inanimate objects can also be affected by transmutation. Examples in the Bible include God turning Moses's and Aaron's staffs into snakes and back to wooden shepherds' sticks (Exodus 7:12). Other significant substance changes involve God turning Lot's wife into a pillar of salt (Genesis 19:26) upon her disobedience to His command and God turning water into blood (Exodus 7:17); and we must not forget that Jesus's first miracle was turning water into wine (John 2:1–11).

If we are to believe those miracles, we must be open to examining the biblical teachings of the resurrection of Christ and His believers. This transmutation of a deceased person into another form is like water being transformed into blood or fine wine through the power of God.

Transmutation is the bedrock of belief in life past death's door. The apostle John writes of how dead seeds bring new life (John 12:24). Buy a packet of seeds from your local hardware store, plant and water them, and you'll see this concept in action.

Here is a challenging but necessary statement: new life always comes from a season of death. Hold on to this biblical promise, and be patient. Something marvelous will blossom after this period of grief.

Transmutation is crucial to reframing our perspective. God's intervention shines through when the world feels dark and hopeless. In seeing something in a new way and gaining a new grip, we begin to see light.

As a Kansas boy, I've learned that severe thunderstorms and tornadoes are part of the natural fabric of growing up on the plains. My parents positioned my bedroom strategically to offer the best protection against the devastating power of a violent windstorm.

Tornadoes exemplify the unpredictability of nature. For those who grew up in Tornado Alley, watching the movie *Twister* (1996) reinforces the power of wind as a destructive force. *Twister* depicts a storm-chasing crew in Oklahoma. The term "twister" is slang for a tornado because the natural phenomenon is a rapidly twisting vortex that typically gains strength as it moves along land, lifting objects large and small off the ground and sometimes displacing them miles from their original location. Animals, vehicles, buildings, and everything in between have been uprooted and thrown miles away.

The film's premise is to release "Dorothy," a device that sends electronically programmed balls into the vortex to flow with the wind stream and transmit data back to the computer so scientists can study the deadly motion/force of what goes on inside a tornado.

While everything appears normal outside that vortex, a new physics system exists within its physical dynamics. Cows and tractor trailers do not fly independently, but within this whirlwind, they can be picked up and carried miles away from their original position. Straw can be driven through cement walls, and metal siding can twist around tree branches—all in a matter of seconds.

Then, just like that, the dynamic force and motion of the wind resumes its normal course, and the energy of the tornado is gone. Meteorologists can detect when the right weather conditions exist for these tornadoes, but they cannot predict when or where one will appear.

This segues nicely into the second form of DAP, motion or force.

Motion/Force

This book functions as a kind of Dorothy, helping us to understand the motion and force of the grieving process. Returning to Exodus and the parting of the Red Sea, this is one of the best biblical examples of force. This action changes the dynamics of the sea, while everything around it appears normal.

The Lord's hand parts the "waters like a wall to them on their right and left" (Exodus 14:29). After all the Israelites have passed between these walls of protection, God allows the waters to resume their course, drowning Pharaoh's army in the process.

In the New Testament, three of the Gospel narratives describe a similar event on the Sea of Galilee in which Jesus Christ demonstrates DAP in relation to acts of nature (Matthew 8:26; Mark 4:39; Luke 8:24). Jesus commands the disciples to cross the Sea of Galilee as a large crowd presses in on them, but a sudden storm catches the disciples off guard. Christ miraculously silences the storm without interfering with the laws of physics beyond His actions.

Here God exercises His dynamic force to chase away our fear of death.

Buoyancy

My first experiential lesson on buoyancy took place while learning to row a canoe when I was thirteen years old, in the First Baptist Church Boy Scout Troop 124. We were taught how to harness our lifejackets before ever getting in the canoe. It was hard to imagine that my 145-pound frame could float.

I learned that buoyancy is the "force exerted on an object that is wholly or partly immersed in a fluid." When any object is submerged, the pressure pushes in on all sides except when the object's weight is less than the pressure from the water; then buoyancy becomes the norm in this natural law.

Divine buoyancy allows people and objects to rise to the surface no matter what weighs them down. The best example lies in the Gospel of Matthew when Jesus walks on the surface of a stormy Sea of Galilee. It is quite possible Jesus walks approximately one mile on the water. He also encourages Peter to step out of the boat and walk on the water—if Peter believes.

Both experience the law of divine buoyancy simultaneously, if only momentarily. As Peter takes his eyes off Christ and starts to worry about what he's doing, he begins to sink. Jesus has to lift him out of the water. Placing Peter back in the nearby boat, Jesus teaches a valuable lesson about keeping focus on Him.

Jesus shows again and again that He extends His miracles to those who place their absolute trust in Christ as the Son of God.

Antigravity

A jet pack is a device worn on the back that uses jets of gas or liquid to propel the wearer through the air. The concept has been present in science fiction for almost a century and became widespread in the 1960s. James Bond uses this technology in the enormously popular movie *Thunderball* (1965) to physically transport to another location and evade pursuing gunmen. The technology continues to be developed and perfected today and has some commercial utility. Modern-day devices use aerodynamic lift to free the wearers from the earth's gravitational pull, lift off, and fly to another location.

With God, individuals can do that without a jet pack.

One of the most fascinating antigravity stories in the Bible is found during the apostle Philip's evangelistic journey in Acts 8:39. Philip is snatched away by an invisible force that deposits him miles away on a desert road. My conclusion is that God uses DAP force to lift Philip and free him from gravity. Antigravity physics also includes the ability to accelerate and land with pinpoint accuracy some thirty-four miles away.

Another movie analogy would be the *Star Trek* teleporter, which can dematerialize a human body, transport it thousands of miles away, and reconstitute it without losing any of the human's physical or mental qualities. The transported human is immediately capable of functioning as though nothing supernatural has occurred.

God, through His infinite wisdom, is gently pulling back the invisible divine curtain of physics for a peek into our eventual resurrection and rapture to God's third realm of Heaven.

In 1935, Albert Einstein and physicist Nathan Rosen developed the theory that space and time are connected through vertical exit and entrance points in two separate dominions. This scientific theory aligns closely with the apostle Paul's reference to the third realm of Heaven (2 Corinthians 12). Paul experienced antigravity through the separation of his soul from his conscious or physical body into the heavenly realm and then was revitalized to return to the earth.

Could it be that Heaven's and Hell's realms exist outside our space-time continuum? Do both exist in separate dimensions with a portal for the angels, Satan, and humans like Paul, Enoch, and Elijah to pass through according to God's will?

Conclusion

Through the multifaceted foundation of transmutation, motion/

force, buoyancy, and antigravity, supernatural signposts proliferate our predictable and natural world order. These signposts prime our spiritual taste buds for the better future coming for all who have placed their faith in Jesus Christ as their Lord and Savior.

During my time providing biblical counseling, I usually asked the "miracle question." This gave someone who was struggling the opportunity to describe whether a miracle happened overnight and if their *big* emotional problem was gone. It was always amazing to hear what relieved their anxiety and what new behaviors brought a healthy lifestyle.

What would this new reality look like for you? Maybe you should ask yourself the miracle question and listen for potential solutions to assist you along this recovery journey.

What would life be like if there were no fear of death? Most likely we would experience a peace and contentment that passes all understanding. Courage means being a risk-taker in moments when we feel paralyzed and helpless; faith in the Lord becomes our substitute until we can find it within ourselves. I love this! It is our opportunity to lean on the strength of the Lord.

Trust me, He has not fallen asleep during our emotional storms; he is right beside us. This insight into God's four supernatural ingredients for miracles helps enhance our God awareness, bringing feelings of safety and trust.

Though my dad would have loved being a storm chaser, he was a storm spotter in real life. Thanks for climbing up on the roof with me to spot the supernatural force of God-driven nature, like my dad did with me years ago. This too symbolizes our Heavenly Father, who desires to take us up to the rooftop—using scripture as our "ladder"—to witness those dynamic forces coming our way.

This might be a good time to grab some cookie dough and enjoy a miracle.

For more answers to your questions or more information, hover over this QR code and follow the link to our website.

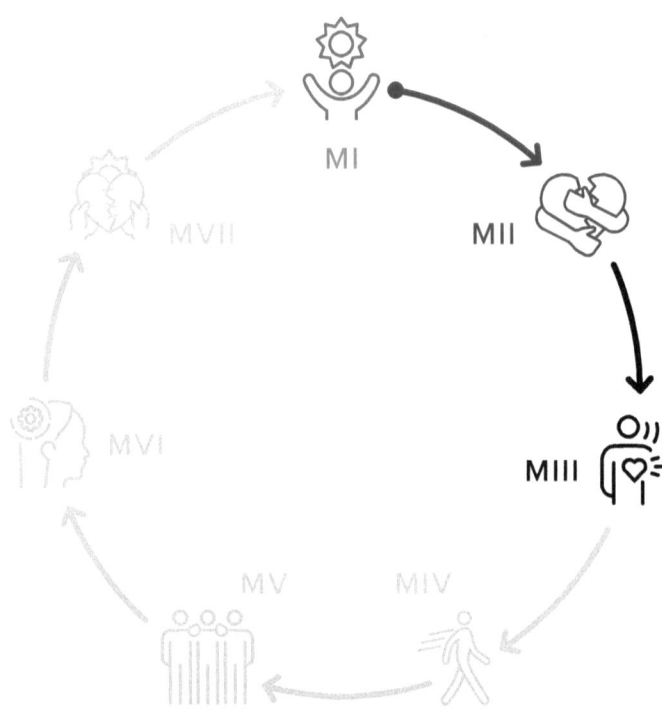

MOVEMENT III: Expressing emotions while listening to your voice as you reflect on positive memories.

MOVEMENT III

Reintegrating Safe & Unsafe Emotions

We have taken two significant steps, like Job, in acknowledging that God gives and takes away by (a) "reassociating" into the moment and (b) "reinforcing" a new mindset of self-care and routines. As Job learned, God uses pain in our lives to serve a greater purpose down the road.

We can perform the third movement by (c) "reintegrating": expressing emotions as we reflect on positive memories and listening to ourselves as we speak with others.

Job moves into firm footing when he hears his friends ruminating over what caused this loss in his life (Job 6:29). Job asks them to adopt another way of thinking that is consistent with how he lived his life with those now gone. Job understands this movement of God in his life not as an attack on his identity and conduct, but instead as a providential sign of God's mysterious will.

Reintegrating with our setting requires us to give voice to our emotions. We may have had this ability prior to our loss, but grief can hijack the ability to be open and honest with raw thoughts and emotions. Listening, comforting, and reflecting on positive accomplishments help give a voice to ourselves and others.

Allow God to add to your self-worth, because you are worthy of His love.

CHAPTER 6

Don't Hush the Message

"I know, my son. I know."

God's Holy Spirit gives us clues, promptings, and inner peace about closing out our earthly lives. During the last few years of my mother's life, she often said, "I am ready to die. I don't know why God has me here."

Not wanting to accept this reality, I advised her to stop talking like that.

Towards the tail end of her years at home, I would drive her to the store in my car. One day, as we idled at a stop sign near her home, she revealed how frustrated she was that three of her siblings had died before her. I tried to express that it was not right to say these things because God has determined our time on this earth. She replied that her dentist had told her she'd outlived her teeth and fillings.

"I am not supposed to live this long," she would lament.

My response was always the same: "Oh, Mom, you shouldn't say things like this."

In His Own Timing

My mother and the biblical Ruth wistfully pleaded, "Why can't I just die? I wasn't supposed to live this long." But God ultimately draws us home in His own timing.

Elisha doesn't struggle to accept Elijah's imminent departure to Heaven when the latter says, "Ask what I can do for you before I am taken from you" (2 Kings 2:9). The former replies, "Let me inherit a double portion of your spirit."

However, previous to that, on two occasions over back-to-back days, the prophets tell Elisha, "Do you know that today the Lord will take your master away from you?" (2 Kings 2:3–5). Each time, Elisha says, "Yes, I know. Be quiet."

This was how I interacted with my mother. I was not ready to acknowledge reality, so I hushed the message.

Two-Way Conversation

When our loved ones talk about leaving us, we should be there to listen and provide positive reinforcement about their accomplishments. But this should be a two-way conversation revealing our own self-awareness at losing a dear loved one. They would probably like to hear that we are open to talking about and processing our fears of their departure. They might need the opportunity to comfort and reassure us of a meaningful future without them.

Releasing Emotional Hurt

The separation should trigger healthy grief, as we see Elisha demonstrate in the action of tearing his clothes in half. This form of mourning symbolizes releasing emotional hurt.

We observe from this narrative that Elisha may have suppressed the outward signs of his fear and unhappiness of losing Elijah. Now he has no choice but to react according to his emotional capacity. Crying and mourning the loss of the relationship is both natural and normal.

Elisha responds appropriately by picking up the purpose God has for him—to carry on the prophetic ministry and message of God to Israel. He asks a great question: not "Where is Elijah?" but "Where is the Lord God of Elijah?"

I hope readers like myself will embrace newfound spiritual insight after tremendous loss. This should be our focus: to live out the presence and witness of God to God's people. If our deceased loved ones were still alive, they would not want us to hush the message; they would want us to lean into the conversation about death.

The Blessings of Not Hushing

One of the best examples of not hushing the message lies in Jacob's final words to his sons in Genesis 47 through 49.

Joseph asks for a final blessing upon his sons, Manasseh and Ephraim. Before blessing his grandsons, Jacob leans in and asks Joseph to place his hand under his father's thigh. Jacob confirms that Joseph has unfailing love towards him and asks Joseph to swear an oath to bury Jacob in Canaan.

However, when Jacob, in his dying moments, blesses the younger son over the firstborn, this displeases Joseph, and he attempts to correct his father. However, Jacob merely states, "I know, my son. I know." He makes his blessings according to God moving in his heart. Joseph suppresses his objection and complies with his dying father's wishes.

When we attempt to correct our loved ones in their last moments, we hush the message.

I have heard from others that their loved ones had one final lucid moment as if prompted by an outside force to speak or smile or somehow reassure their loved ones that they knew death was moments away.

The Moment of Releasing the Hush

This was the case in my last moments alone with Mom in her room.

My brothers had left for home, and I stayed longer. I still remember the room, her bed, and the look on her face; it was the look of someone who was not fully aware, sedated by morphine. She lay lifeless for days after her major stroke, with no sign of movement other than her breathing.

I shut the door to her room, bent down next to her bed, and reassured her that my life was going well and my boys had a bright future. I told her she was a wonderful mom to me and a terrific grandmother to my children. In that moment, my soul knew that Mom would not make it. Soon—maybe after another day or so, according to the hospice nurse—she would pass. This was my moment to be real. Holding her hand, I sobbed. I did not want her to die, but I also didn't want her to suffer anymore. I am not sure how long or how loud I cried, but a wonderful thing happened.

Mom lifted her head and opened her eyes to look right at me one last time. She wanted to know who was crying at her bedside. She then slowly lay back down, returning to her still state.

I stopped crying, stunned at this gesture of love and concern over my weeping. I had seen it before when I was growing up. This was her moment of telling me, "I know, my son. I know."

We must not hush our thoughts, feelings, and overwhelming sadness. Our loved ones need to hear it; it draws them close to us as they stand in death's doorway. We stay present to meet their last needs but also to allow them to meet our needs as we say goodbye for now. I would rather my mom pass amid my love and tears than have her be numb to how God closes out our lives in front of our grieving loved ones.

The Spirit helps us release our deep emotions so that both parties gain a meaningful moment of closeness. To be comforted and know that we are loved when passing into the Lord's arms is amazingly significant and intimate.

Honoring Loved One's Last Wishes

At the end, we should reassure our loved ones of the future we will carry on, like they did when their siblings or parents passed away. We can honor the hush by fulfilling their desires for burial arrangements and living out their values and the best parts of who they are in our daily lives. We can keep their legacies and memory alive.

CHAPTER 7

A Grave Interest

"Grief is valor in spiritual warfare."

For most, Memorial Day signaled the opening of the municipal swimming pool and the official arrival of summer. But this was not the case for my family. For us, this was a time of drudgery.

Every Memorial Day during my childhood, the family appeased my mom by helping her visit the grave sites of her loved ones. Helping consisted of pulling all the memorial flowers down from the garage attic, which meant backing out the car, setting up the large ladder, and pushing open the attic's sheet-rock covering. For crawling into the attic in the May heat and locating all the memorial flower boxes, a three-man crew was needed—one in the attic, one on the ladder, and one on the floor receiving the boxes.

Finally, we took the trip to Mount Hope Cemetery in Mount Hope, Kansas. We grumbled as we helped Mom load the flowers. Dad and I shared the same thoughts about how Memorial Day should be honored: *anything* was preferable to taking all day to go to the cemetery. We often had similar thoughts about life.

In the blistering heat, Mom would coach us in precisely placing each flower by the headstones of her two brothers, Harold and Robert, as well as those of her parents. Once the flowers were perfectly laid out, we squinted directly into the sun as our pictures were taken with a Canon AF35ML camera. Reshoots were often required due to the lens cap being left on or a finger slipping over the lens.

My mother had a "grave" interest in visiting her loved ones. In my youth, I could not understand why we needed to honor a bunch of headstones. This question was finally answered when I became an adult. Mom did not talk much about the dead, but when I asked who they were and what was so interesting about their lives, Mom would reveal her memories of them. Each story would end with "I will see them again."

As she aged into her late seventies, even though Mom's body became frail, she was the same person underneath the skin.

It seems that the dimming light in our eyes is indicative of that promise made in Genesis 3:19: "returning to dust."

Do It When Ready

We are ready to visit the grave when we want to go back and see the grave. If we do not want to go back, we are not ready. When we are ready, we should be intentional about when we go and why—not because others expect us to go every Memorial Day.

Visiting the graveside is not time and energy wasted but rather an investment in the memories that have meaning and value.

Do It with Meaning

Leaving items at gravesides has been practiced by Jews for many centuries. This practice helped lead to the permanent headstones we have today.

Placing a symbolic item on the grave reminds us that we are emotionally tethered to our loved ones. If they were alive to see the intimate gesture, it would warm their hearts.

Do It to Share Their Legacy with Others

Each visit to the grave is another opportunity to connect with the personhood of the loved one—their personality, things they laughed about, positive memories, etc.

This brief connection to their past life can motivate us to communicate the impact this person had on our lives and their unique perspective on life's problems. Passing on lessons from those who loved us and whom we loved leaves a true legacy in the lives of the next generation.

Do It as Worship

Grief gives honor to God.

In the grip of pain following the death of his children, Job is exhorted by his wife to speak unkindly towards God—to "blaspheme." It can be tempting to vent our anger towards Him, but this is not the way to move past it. Job understands that good and bad things all come from God, and he makes the hard decision to accept His will. Job silences his lips. This is true worship when life goes sideways.

Prior to Job's loss, God offered His servant to Satan in a cosmic battle of faith that would become a lesson for the ages. This is the bloodiest spiritual combat we face: protecting the holy ground of our hearts. Grief is valor in spiritual warfare. Accepting and working through our pain takes courage. Remember, the battle belongs to the

Lord, who gives us victory over sin, pain, loneliness, and even death.

Mom's last trip to the cemetery did not go well. She got confused when turning left through a major intersection, second-guessed herself, and ended up on the sidewalk. No one was hurt, but the incident caused traffic issues. The police were called to the scene of the accident, and in her mental state, Mom struggled to be polite and responsive. They recognized some cognitive and motor skill impairments.

This well-intended trip to pick up Memorial Day flowers for Dad's gravestone ended Mom's independent living. Her last time driving a car was to go across town to pick up those eternal, plastic flowers. Her heart's desire was to remember by showing her love and appreciation for the moments precious to them both.

The ability to visit the grave will help us express and heal unsafe emotions by giving them voice. There are two voices that need to connect: the voice of our unsafe emotions and the voice of our love, communicating those faith values. Two voices, one faith.

CHAPTER 8

The Lewis Life

"For us to grieve well may require us to learn the art of switch-foot surfing."

While my oldest son loves to attend concerts and can provide plenty of biographical details and information on intra-band drama, I am not a concertgoer. However, one concert changed my life significantly.

In 2001, my close friend Lewis went home to be with the Lord on Easter Sunday. His passing was sudden and traumatic to both family and friends.

When the funeral ceremony concludes, we often deceive ourselves into thinking that our emotional and cognitive pain is over for now; we might not adequately mourn the loss. As in a middle school boy's gym locker, our emotions fester like the gym clothes we forget to take home for a good laundering. Opening the hurt locker a week later reveals that our dirty laundry has not magically disappeared. Out of sight is not out of heart.

Back to the concert. The band was about one song into the set when I began to connect the lyrics with the emotion of my loss. Under the cloud of loud music, I wept out all my sharp-edged grief from that hurt locker.

The band's headline song was about not wanting to wait for the future resurrection but instead wanting to embrace the resurrection power now!

I needed to be reminded that the resurrection of my friend was fact. My friend lived out the resurrection power in his daily life. This concert provided healing and allowed me to reframe my life to live out the "Lewis life" of Christ to others. God brought Lewis into my life for nearly six months, and I look forward to seeing him in glory.

As we work to clarify the object of this chapter, we must remember that death is the natural release from our earthly abode, enabling us to be eternally present with the Lord (2 Corinthians 5:1–6). As humans, we are unable to summon divine action. Only God can do this, and He will act in His own timing.

Lewis was a faithful participant in my Sunday school class. He had a profound way of processing spiritual thought. One Sunday, I was teaching Philippians 3:10–13, which talks about the power of the resurrection in our daily lives. We were studying how this connects to the apostle Paul. Sharing the message of Christ to the Praetorian Guards who are chained to him while he is in Rome under house arrest, Paul focuses on what lies ahead rather than lamenting what has happened in the past (Philippians 3:13).

Lewis spoke up: "Well, if I share Christ and they become Christians, then I win. If they take my life due to Christ's message, then I win. Either way, I win!"

Lewis quickly grasped the work of the Holy Spirit in his life. He understood from the outset that sharing Christ in our mortal bodies is to live for Christ, and if our persecutors kill us before the Holy Spirit wins them over, then our death is a gain. As believers, we need a solid grasp of the resurrection narratives to be comforted by the Word of God. To live a Lewis life of boldness with those around us is to win.

A few crucial principles within Jesus's resurrection narrative will forge an understanding of death being a gain. It may not make sense now, but it will.

This Lewis life connects to our cookie dough concept back in chapter 5. Just as the aroma of freshly baked chocolate chip cookies fills the air with a sweet smell, the miracle of Jesus's resurrection points to something special and marvelous for us to enjoy: this pending supernatural encounter with God.

And just as some chocolate chip cookies have almonds, some peanut butter, and some oatmeal, there are also variations in the theology of resurrection—specifically, three.

In previous chapters, we discussed the conflict between creative order and divine action physics. We concluded that this "conflict" came from the disbelief that God can create a dynamic system that includes temporal, interim, and imperishably resurrected bodies.

These three components are rooted in both Old and New Testament narratives.

Temporal Divine Action Resurrection Physics

In First Kings 17:17–24, Elijah the Tishbite heals the dead son of a widow in Zarephath. Elijah lays across the dead boy three times while praying for God to raise him back to life. Life is restored to the child as a testimony of God's power during a reigning pagan culture.

As we read in Second Kings 4:18–37, Elisha also brings a dead child back to life, in Shunem. Like Elijah, Elisha places himself on the dead child while pleading for God's power to raise the dead. The boy's heart is revived, and blood begins to flow. This child has also tasted death but is revived to his original human condition. When the boy's mother sees him alive, she bows and worships God. Unable to contain her joy, she rushes out to share the miraculous power of Elisha's God.

Our next example of temporal resurrection is found in the

thirteenth chapter of John with the resurrection of Jesus's dear friend Lazarus. Jesus is likely at least one full day's walk from Bethany when He receives news of his friend's mortal sickness. Upon arriving at the burial site, Jesus calls to Lazarus, who stumbles out of the tomb wrapped in the death cloth. Lazarus returns to his family to live out his life after suffering a physical death. He dies again later, but he is not afraid because he knows there is life beyond the grave.

Our final example of temporal divine action physics directly relates to the timing of Christ's death in Jerusalem. In the moment Jesus gives up His spirit, Matthew tells us the temple curtain is supernaturally torn, the earth shakes, and saints long dead and buried in the tombs come back to life. They walk out of their death sleep and are physically alive once again (Matthew 25:52, 53).

Like Lazarus, the saints in Jerusalem experience restorative resurrection. Their original blood is restored and their bones revitalized. Due to this being a temporal divine action intervention, these postdeath saints are recognizable to family members and carry on their earthly lives in relationships—eating, sleeping, and eventually dying a second time.

In each of these narratives, people taste death but experience a revived human life through the miraculous work of God. I wonder what kind of testimony these renewed saints would share with their living loved ones about their victory over death. Although it might be a bummer to die a second time, I am convinced they all had the confidence to live boldly for Christ, knowing that death is merely a portal to the divine presence of God!

It is now through the death of Christ—before His resurrection—that believers are released from the grip of death. I am not afraid of death but rather emboldened in my faith through the work of the cross, knowing what awaits me on the other side.

Interim Divine Action Resurrection

This brings us to the interim divine action. What qualifies?

"Interim" implies a segment of time between two events. Here the two events are the earthly resurrection and Christ's ascension in Acts chapter 1.

Christ is in His postdeath metamorphosis. His earthly body has been resurrected but in an advanced physical temporal status. Unlike temporal divine action, the interim divine action resurrection transforms the body into a postdeath state. The blood and bone composites are different, so divine action physics can be applied, allowing the body to pass through material substances and consume food. However, the face and physical features became unrecognizable to those in the inner circle of relationships. Even the voice changes.

Like with temporal restoration, Christ continues to eat and sleep and carry on normal human activities: setting a fire and frying fish for the apostles, then eating that meal with them is one example. Unlike Lazarus in John 11, Jesus retains His personhood and His deity. However, His earthly, limited body is permanently transformed! He will not have to face death again like those who experience temporal divine action.

In essence, Christ has broken the impervious trigger of death, reversing the one-way door.

This death trigger is a supernatural point of resistance that does not allow those who have died to reset their biological clock. Life has a preset time of "slack" where it travels through time. Regardless of how hard a person works to be healthy, no one can reset the slack preceding that death trigger. Leading up to the trigger's release, our resistance builds, causing the body to age and struggle with functional health issues.

This law of divine intervention is not a reciprocal mechanism in which the law of creative order can jump or leapfrog into the other realm. The natural portal is death, but within the time appointed by our sovereign God, the trigger of death is employed for His purpose.

The joy is that our newly raised body will be Spirit filled—no longer coupled with the earthly realm, no longer controlled by the natural laws of aging, sickness, or disease. As Paul says in First Corinthians 15:50–58: "Death has been swallowed up in victory!"

The final movement of reintegration involves stitching the supernatural patch of the resurrection on our hearts. In time, we will feel safe in knowing that Christ is in control of our deaths and the deaths of those we love.

Here's my task for you today: try to express your emotions about your spiritual pain—to God and those who love you and whom you love. You can choose not to express your pain in a crowd of strangers but rather find the right outlet for the emotional valve to be released. You can allow God to stitch on the life-after-death patch now. This patch of God's supernatural work opens the path for Him to speak to our hearts.

What does He want to say to us in the moment? He desires to draw us close and speak grace into our self-worth. We are worthy of this patch. Christ earned it so we can live without fear of death. Why would God do this? Simply, He wants us with Him in eternity. Wow!

We are worthy of His love.

Several years ago, while at a convention in San Diego, I had the chance to walk the famous Oceanside Pier. The massive, wooden pier was a great place to watch the surfers ride the waves in front of the crowd on the beach. Many of the surfers washed out before ever making it to the beach. Occasionally, one would ride the waves all the way to the beach, and the onlookers would express their excitement through cheering and applause. I noticed that the successful surfers were able to pivot their boards in the opposite direction several times due to the waves. As I looked closer, I realized these surfers were quickly rotating their left feet to the rear so their right feet ended up in a forward position. I asked a few young men watching with me on the pier, and they explained that this is called switch-foot surfing.

Grief is like the waves of the sea. They tend to roll in on us suddenly, twisting and bending, testing our faith. For us to grieve well may require us to learn the art of switch-foot surfing. When emotions swell like waves on our hearts, they are controlled by unconscious undercurrents of thoughts that rapidly change direction, throwing us off balance. Like surfing, switch-foot grieving pivots towards the source of changing emotions as they occur.

The wave of joyful fulfillment is coming, so be ready to switch your feet on the longboard of faith and take the most thrilling ride of your life. Just like Lewis, you will begin to see how God brings grace, hope, blessings, miracles, and truth to your life. Keeping training, as God continues to stitch on the life-after-death patch on your heart.

For more answers to your questions or more information, hover over this QR code and follow the link to our website.

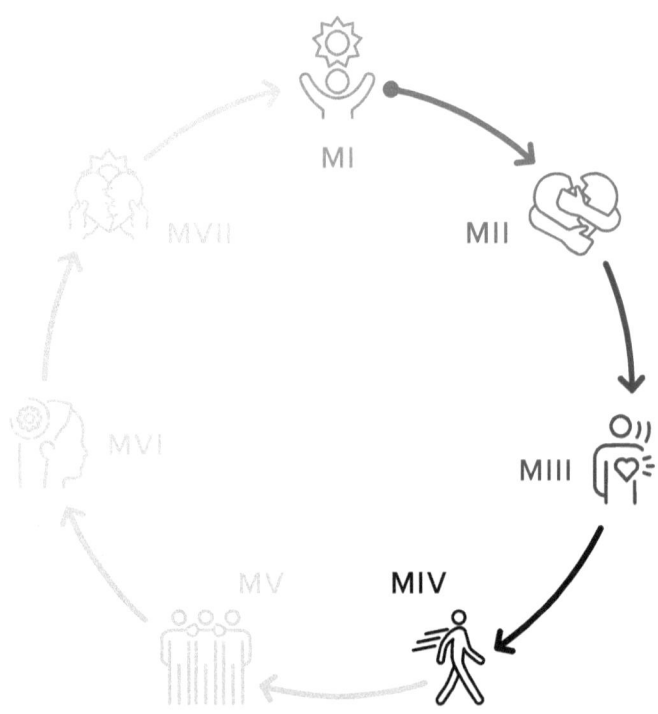

MOVEMENT IV: Acknowledging past behavior as sufficient by focusing on positive movements vs. regrets.

MOVEMENT IV

Reaffirming Past Behavior

Music cuts through time, connecting us with a moment or person associated with a given tune. Maybe it triggers a brief flash of memory where we can smell, feel, taste, and reexperience that moment.

When it comes up, I do not want to run from it. I want to dance. I want to bask in that experience again. The love we remember flows back. That is what makes hearing that music so painful at the beginning but so much more meaningful as the last note hangs in the air.

This relates to our fourth movement, which is the ability to "reaffirm" our past conduct towards our loved ones by focusing on the positive moments versus the deadly pit of regret. So, how do we dance around the edges of regret?

We again look to Job, in his response to the second round of discussions, where he stands by his past conduct as righteous (Job 17:9). Standing by our past conduct doesn't mean we think we were perfect in all of our choices but that, with the Lord's direction, we did the best we could to make the right decisions in our time with our loved ones.

When we begin to reaffirm, we must work through thoughts of regret, such as "I should have spent more time with them," "I should have done more," or "I should have been there." These kinds of thoughts will not help us dance through the grief music. We must accept the past.

It was what it was.

It is what it is.

CHAPTER 9

Divine Intervention Physics

"God is our lifeguard who shows up in ways we cannot explain or rationalize."

I did not like science growing up. It was confusing, and only the smart kids understood how to plant a peanut seed or dissect a frog without throwing up.

Despite my distaste for physics, I of course experienced the effects of gravity as a small child, in reenactments of the *Six Million Dollar Man* from the top of my fence or jumping over trash cans in the spirit of Evil Knievel on my earthbound banana-seat bike.

As we mature and grow through life phases such as independent adulthood, marriage, and parenthood, we realize that God is active in meeting not only our physical needs but also our thirsty, dry, and ragged souls. God has a master plan combining the natural and the divine to fulfill His will in our lives.

Jesus mentioned that we are more important than the sparrows. If God provides for a sparrow who needs a worm to feed her babies, He will certainly take care of our physical and spiritual needs. God's providential care is apparent throughout His creation—through our experiences of seeing our children born, shuffling off to kindergarten, and eventually driving away to college, for example. We often fail to see how active God is in our lives, but once we glimpse His movement, we realize that cutting a blade of grass, shoveling a driveway, or putting a Band-Aid on a child's skinned-up knee all point to His providential love. There is a God, and we have a soul that thirsts for Him. And he deeply cares about our grief and the emotional trauma of losing a loved one.

David, the psalmist, declares in Psalm 139 that God saw his unformed body and all his deeds in the flesh before birth. God knitted us together with the care of a master weaver. We were not a mistake, nor did God leave out anything He wanted to create in His image.

David is clearly saying, "You were born broken, and you will not remain in brokenness." It is a fact that we have a loving Father who created us to seek and enjoy Him even after our earthly passing.

That the warmest love to ever exist will radiate in our hearts in our new eternal home should be comforting. Regardless of how long we live, our earthly life will eventually end. We will have an opportunity to see our loved ones again, in vibrant health and new bodies, never to die again. We read about this in the Bible, but we do not generally make the connection that our name will soon be listed in the Book of Death alongside billions of other people who went before us and will come after us.

According to the Bible, only two men ever escaped death: Enoch ("Enoch walked with God, and he was not, for God took him," from Genesis 5:23–24); and Elijah ("And as they still went on and talked, behold, chariots of fire and horses of fire separated the two of them. And Elijah went up by a whirlwind into heaven," from 2 Kings 2:11).

I wonder whether our grief would run the gamut from horror to amazement if we watched our loved ones get swooped up by a golden chariot of fire to disappear into the clouds. Would we celebrate for joy? Would we be overwhelmed with fear? God could have made this the norm, but this is not His divine will for us. Those were exceptional circumstances, with God choosing to break the natural order for those two men, Enoch and Elijah.

The desire for meaning and purpose in our lives and the reality of death point us to God's next step for us: to experience the physics of God's intervention past the door of death and enter eternal life.

When I was eighteen, I attended the National Baptist Youth Conference in Rhode Island. I was selected to lead a small discipleship group of twelve high school students from across the country for one week at Brown University. During our break from the conference, we could sign up for sightseeing tours around Rhode Island. One such trip was to the beach.

I was naive and young, in a strange place without family members to watch out for me and with newfound freedom. A parent keeps an eye on their child in the water and on personal belongings such as towels, shoes, clothing, eyeglasses, and watches. But being alone and excited about swimming in the ocean and riding the waves for the first time, I didn't take such considerations. The concept of the current dragging me down the beach from my starting point did not cross my mind. Before I knew what had happened, I was several thousand yards away. Without my glasses, I could not see my original beach spot. The thousands of towels on the beach all looked the same, and a sudden terror overcame me.

While I was searching for my belongings, a bullhorn announced that my bus was leaving in ten minutes. A second wave of terror filled me. I worried I would be abandoned in the Atlantic Ocean with thousands of strangers in an unfamiliar place. And I could not figure out where my glasses, towel, and street clothes were.

I asked for the Lord's help in finding my belongings. Suddenly, a blur shaped like a female lifeguard asked if I needed help. I said, "Yes," describing my belongings and my inability to see farther than my hands.

It was such a relief to find someone who was trying to help me! Still, I thought it would be impossible to locate everything in a timely manner. This lifeguard had me follow her, and she took the lead up the beach, soon pausing over a pile of stuff.

She asked, "Is this it?"

I bent down and located my glasses in my shoes and put them on immediately. When I looked up to thank her, she was gone.

I have no idea what she looked like or where she came from, but to me, that she walked me directly to my belongings several thousand yards up the beach was a miracle. Was she an angel? I strongly believe she was and that, for a moment, I experienced the intervention of God.

What would God's purpose have been in the intervention and divine action? My only thought is that God was using me as a vessel for those I was teaching at the youth conference. God was moving within those students who would be leaving for college and needed the confidence to be bold witnesses to their friends on campus. God intervened to say, "I care about you, Terry," and "I care about the ministry of my Word to my followers."

I would have been stranded and unable to function or return to Brown University from the beach. The times when we are helpless, lack vision, and feel emotionally overwhelmed are where God meets us. God wants to commune with us, especially in moments of shock and loss. On that beach, I could have wandered for hours and never found my belongings. But divine intervention moves without restrictions, through time and space, in this case looking over every object on that big beach so that, in a matter of minutes, that angelic "lifeguard" could walk me directly to my belongings.

Could this event be reproduced with the same speed and accuracy? Maybe not. I immediately knew something supernatural had occurred in my life; if it happened again, it would not be as miraculous. This is an example of why miracles cannot be reproduced.

Several weeks after the conference's conclusion, nearly all the group participants sent letters thanking me for helping them see God's work in their lives. While it was for His glory that He intervened, God kept me on schedule to teach the small group and prevented me from missing the bus and getting distracted, frustrated, and discouraged. There was a larger purpose here, and God continues to minister through me with this story today.

God is our lifeguard who shows up in ways we cannot explain or rationalize. We likely all have at least one or two secret stories of providence tucked away in our souls. His infinite purpose for us is revealed through divine interventions, specific portals into our lives where natural order is suspended and the supernatural steps into the moment like a divine lifeguard.

Though I am not wired to enjoy the sciences, I know God has a master plan that intertwines the natural and the divine to fulfill His will in our lives.

For more answers to your questions or more information, hover over this QR code and follow the link to our website.

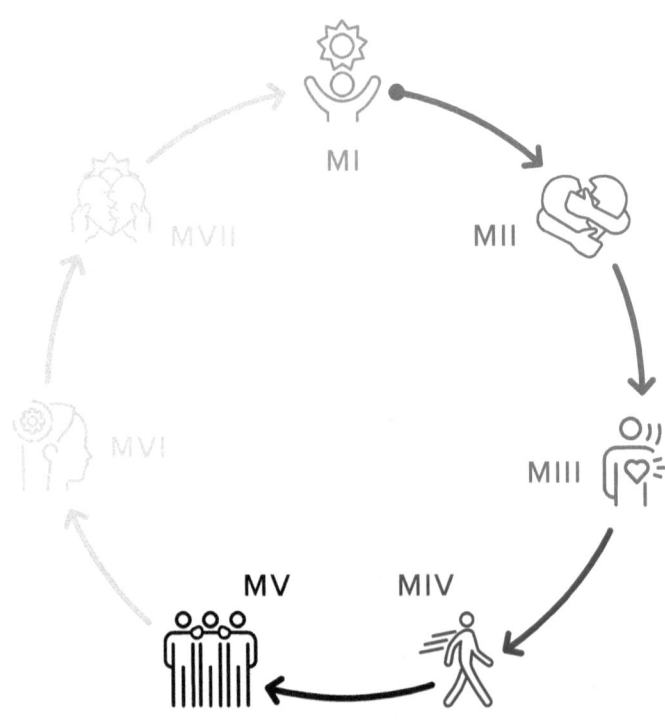

MOVEMENT V: Leaning on supportive relationships that foster godly worth.

MOVEMENT V

Restoring Your Grip

In July of 1981, I was in a hitting slump on my eighth-grade summer baseball team. After some coaching from my dad, combined with my best impression of a George Brett batting stance, I had improved my hitting to .350 as a lead-off batter, but something else happened that took my mind off the game.

I remember it clearly. Two overhead walkways at the Hyatt Regency Hotel in Kansas City collapsed on July 17, killing 114 people. Watching the suffering of the victims' families on TV did something to me. Today this is called vicarious trauma: trauma absorbed through other's suffering and loss, projected onto ourselves.

My mom understood the connection between what I saw on TV and my worsening game. She reached out to my older brother Roger, a former pitcher, about the situation.

Roger showed up at our home one Saturday without warning and took me to a local baseball field. He pitched balls for hours, and I hit them. We both spent time shagging balls in the field, then did it all over again. My hitting came back. I got back into my groove, hitting like little George Brett Jr.!

Roger's support through a meaningful activity made all the difference. I will never forget how he made me feel important, worthy of care, and valuable. Roger helped me understand and make sense of the tragedy in KC. Job experiences this same moment when God sends "mediators" who are gracious to his hurting heart and speak into the process of restoration. I love how Ehilu speaks of the sovereignty of God with words like "be gracious," "spare him," "a ransom," "renewed," and "restored" (Job 33:25, 26).

My baseball swing was restored by spending meaningful time with my brother doing what brought me pleasure and joy. Even though that day with Roger was but a brief moment, it gave me hope for more joy in the future. I envisioned a future of hitting again as I regained my focus and confidence, thanks to a friendly gesture from my brother.

This is what supportive relationships do. They assist in the process of restoring our godly worth and sense of meaning and hope for our future.

CHAPTER 10

Two Scoops of Comfort

"A glimpse of God's inner workings shows us everything will be okay and nothing is as bad as we think."

I recently traveled to France on a bucket-list trip. So many cool and meaningful stories came from this trip. My experience of being a visitor in a strange land changed me.

I could speak a few words in French and translate using a wonderful app on my phone; however, I had a frustrating experience at a Paris train station. Understanding the digital travel board was fairly easy. The problem was that the information about which gate our train would depart from and which train we needed to board was inaccurate. This required asking for help.

My travel guide persistently asked station personnel for assistance. Each time, they randomly pointed to another fluorescent-jacketed staff member who knew no more than the first person. This "shake-off" was frustrating because time was ticking.

This is how it feels to be a foreign traveler on a journey with little or no help from people who know the answers. We were desperate to find someone who could speak our language and guide us. Discovering that person was a joyful moment because the stress of traveling was somewhat relieved by the relative assurance of getting to the right place at the right time.

The grieving process creates a similar confusion—another language barrier of sorts and frustration at time running out. We are traveling down an unfamiliar path, and no one seems to understand or speak our grief language. When we do find someone who speaks to our hurting heart, we feel comforted, like me finding another English-speaking person in a non-English-speaking country.

The good news is that we are not traveling on this healing journey alone. Comfort is available.

Paul writes in chapter 1 of Second Corinthians of the abundance of God's comfort in our lives. This comfort is made up of two words: *para* (meaning "alongside") and *klesis* ("calling to one's aid"). Comfort can thus be envisioned as one who is called to another person for encouragement.

Paul also describes God as the source of compassion ("mercy"). Since God is the source of both compassion and comfort, it is His responsibility or obligation to dispense these to those wrestling with affliction (2 Corinthians 1:3).

God is invested in our spiritual and emotional well-being. This is evident in the word "salvation" that Paul uses to bring relief and well-being to our souls (2 Corinthians 1:6). God can and does speak our language, and he will guide us through our suffering and get us on the train heading in the right direction. How does this impact our emotional distress? This comfort of God "energizes" our minds to be resolute and expectant of a meaningful future.

What are the effects of this comfort in our lives? The divine action of God's comfort is released through the saving knowledge of Christ's work on the cross, providing an inner revitalization that imbues us with divine strength to make it through the day. When we see God providing energy for us to take one step at a time, our perspective changes from that of a lost stranger to that of a traveler enjoying the rolling green pastures from the train window.

God's comfort gives strength and perspective, showing how far we have come since our loss. This divine endurance is the result of God not allowing us to give up on our own lives.

How do we access this divine endurance? By taking in the comfort God offers and giving out the same comfort we receive to others. This is the essence of spiritual well-being.

Spiritual Well-Being Framework

Traumatic Spiritual Event

Steadfast Frame of Mind

Inward — Taking In
- Listening
- Learning
- Internalizing
- Leaning On

Comfort Of God

Outward — Giving Out
- Listening
- Learning
- Leaning In
  - Shift to Need
  - Praying for Healing

This comfort emboldens and strengthens our faith in Christ. Our faith grows deeper and more resilient to adversity. As the action agent of change, Jesus Christ is the vehicle for comfort.

Here is how it works.

Comfort can be intermittent, meaning that it comes and goes during our emotional cycle. God wants us to understand that our pain does not vanish instantly when we make that request. This short pause in grief tips us off to what precipitated this short burst of comfort. Perhaps it was a meaningful hymn, a brief phone call from a friend, or a card in the mail. A friend might recognize that we simply need a hug.

We must not dismiss this burst of comfort but instead embrace it!

One day, we might wake up and desire to do something meaningful or fun. When we can go through a full day without thinking of our loss, this means God has intervened in our pain and our spiritual well-being is coming back online. This could happen suddenly and without notice. Motivation might come from someone simply sitting down and speaking our language.

God's comfort is not bound by the natural laws of physics. He can cross over the boundaries of physics whenever He chooses, providing comfort to make every day better and better. Another way of looking at this is His divine force acts on our hearts and minds, renewing our spirits day by day. One week is better than the first day, and one month is better than the first week. The process is one of growth and regeneration prompted by God's choice.

Practical Principles of Comfort

God absorbs our inner spirit when we work through His Word, listen to His voice, learn vital lessons, and internalize His work in us. We can accomplish this easily by listening to an audio Bible. Listening to a narrator speak God's Word has a calming effect.

We can also attend a small-group Bible study or a Sunday school class. We may not feel like it, but it creates opportunities to embrace God's comforting words. We can internalize through journaling or making audio recordings of our daily thoughts, struggles, and successes. This helps us reflect on our emotional journeys.

We can also find comfort by becoming aware of others in need. Comfort is two sided: internal and external. When God puts us in front of someone who has physical or emotional needs, we might pause our personal pain to listen to their story. Letting them speak, learning from them, and leaning into what that special moment requires can bring us all comfort.

Recently, I learned that a friend's mother had been placed in hospice. This provided an amazing opportunity to pull up a chair, hold her hand, and give comfort back to someone who was dying. Keep in mind, I had not been there for a person like this since my mom died.

No fear and only love, joy, and kindness flowed from my heart to "Mom." We laughed, we sang, and we told stories of God's faithfulness in our lives. This was me leaning in and embracing God's comfort more than five years ago.

This can be you someday if God desires a similar opportunity for you. Paul says clearly in Philippians chapter 2 to look out for the interests of others. When these two divine actions are combined, a steadfast frame of mind develops. Then a new perspective emerges as it relates to the past event. A glimpse of God's inner workings shows us everything will be okay and nothing is as bad as we think.

As an experienced overseas traveler now, I empathize with those who are lost and lack direction in our neck of the woods. I know what it is like to feel anxiety, frustration, and sometimes panic when I get on the wrong path. I am changed by the small tokens of kindness and encouragement I received in France.

This is how the comfort of God works. He comforts me when I suffer so I can comfort others who are suffering (2 Cor. 1:3-4). In fact, my experience of God's comfort is as abundant as my experience of loss and pain in this life.

I will bone up on French and learn from this experience so that when I return, I can help others.

PS: My sweet spot is at the Crème de la Paris Ice Cream. Shop and watch the sun set over the Notre Dame de Paris! "Two scoops, please, on a waffle cone!"

For more answers to your questions or more information, hover over this QR code and follow the link to our website.

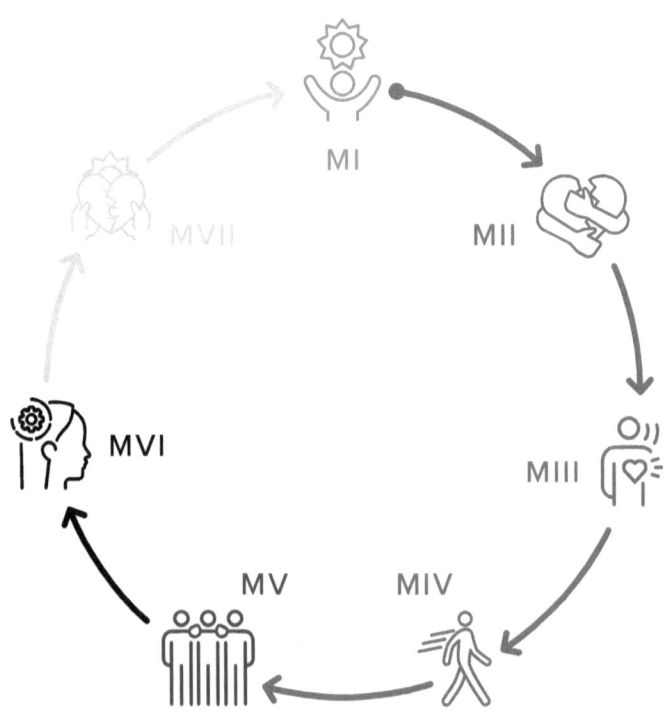

MOVEMENT VI: Adjusting to life without the past relationship.

MOVEMENT VI
Recalibrating by Adjusting

I recently took up a new sport: e-biking. Until I started driving at sixteen, I rode my banana bike and ten-speed all over town. I had forgotten how much I enjoyed bicycling; the freedom, wind, warm sunshine, and light exercise made me feel good.

Moving from a traditional bike to an electric bike (a bike with a battery) requires some recalibration. Speed is no longer contingent upon exertion. An e-bike adjusts to your pedaling and determines how much force is needed on the wheels for longer rides or navigating hills. This makes riding an e-bike almost effortless.

When we go through tough changes, we tend to rely on old skills and thinking. This movement away from old thinking is similar to e-biking, as both require adjusting to a new reality without the former relationship. Though not on a traditional bike, I am still on two wheels, holding on to handlebars, and pedaling. The conventional bike isn't there, but the structure, feeling, and enjoyment is the same.

When we recalibrate from a physical separation, the ability to continue down life's path is energized by positive memories and how they shaped us into who we are. This new understanding propels us to enjoy the ride. Keep in mind that those we lost, especially those older than us, also had to recalibrate from the loss of their loved ones, yet they continued to give us joy, support, and meaning.

Remember Job? He said that he could really see God. He did this by changing his mind about blaming God for the loss of his children. He said, "I know that you can do all things; no purpose of yours can be thwarted" (Job 42:2).

This spiritual recalibration requires us to turn towards the face of Christ to really see God. The face of Christ attaches us to God's supernatural battery, helping us pedal through life's abrupt turns. We no longer move forward with abandonment but instead consciously enjoy the warmth of Christ's love releasing us back into that childlike joy of positive memories.

To recalibrate is to accept that God chooses not to give us full understanding of the why, preferring us to mature in the glory of Christ that propels us down a new path of life.

CHAPTER 11

The Final Frontier

"We never know when God will show up on the front porch of our hearts."

I am a huge fan of pop-culture hero Captain James T. Kirk of *Star Trek* fame. Twisting the antennae on our black-and-white TV to capture the signal was an art and a science. When we eventually broke the plastic knob on the channel bolt, red-handled pliers did the job. Spock would have been proud of us.

We were drawn into the imagination of Eugene Wesley Roddenberry in the late 1960s. The technology that assisted the USS *Enterprise* was astounding. We drank in the concepts of time and space travel and were fascinated by communicator devices, telepresence, tricorders, cool phasers, tractor beams, and, oh yes, warp drive.

The transporter is one of the most exciting gadgets on Starship *Enterprise*. Seeing Captain Kirk teleport into an enemy camp while riding a motorcycle is a real thrill. Unfortunately, the science behind this one is complicated. But TV audiences have been captivated ever since seeing a character get beamed up for the first time.

The transporter was originally conceived as a device to convey characters from a starship to the surface of a planet without the need for expensive and time-consuming special effects to depict the starship or another craft physically landing. Transporters convert a person or object into an energy pattern (a process called "dematerialization"), then send ("beam") it to a target location, where it is reconverted into matter ("rematerialization").

Star Trek: Final Frontier shows a fictional account of humans flying into outer space and reveals humans' enormous fascination with outer space and capabilities beyond our current human capacity.

Death is not our final frontier. It presents no emotional or physical threat if we place our hope and faith in Christ. It becomes a transformation into a new beginning.

To prepare us for this mindset, we will look at two basic laws of physics to build a solid foundation in understanding how God works and functions in this world and beyond. God's universal order encompasses both natural and divine reality.

God invented four natural sciences (physics, chemistry, astronomy, geoscience/biology) to reflect His glory through His creation.

- Physics is the science of matter, involving the study of its fundamental constituents, its motion and behavior through space and time, and the related entities of energy and force. Physics is one of the most fundamental scientific disciplines, with its main goal being to understand how the universe behaves. A scientist who specializes in the field of physics is called a physicist.
- Chemistry is the scientific study of the properties and behavior of matter. It covers substances (elements and compounds): their composition, structure, properties, behavior, and the changes they undergo during a reaction with other substances. Chemistry also addresses the nature of chemical bonds in chemical compounds.
- Astronomy is one of the oldest scientific disciplines, and it has evolved from the humble beginnings of counting stars and

charting constellations with the naked eye to the impressive showcase of technological capabilities we see today.
- Geoscience is the study of the earth—our oceans, atmosphere, rivers and lakes, ice sheets and glaciers, soils, complex surface, rocky interior, and metallic core. This includes many aspects of how living things, including humans, interact with the earth. Geoscience has many tools and practices of its own but is intimately linked with the biological, chemical, and physical sciences.

God also created divine physics, which has no boundaries or constraints and operates outside the aforementioned groupings of natural sciences.

Natural science lies within the scientific law of creative order (LCO). Another form of physics within this universal order is what I've called divine action physics (DAP). A protective "bubble" allows DAP to operate without disrupting the physical structure of LCO. This "intervention" or divine intervention helps to express depth within God's creative order.

Remember the scene from the 2009 reboot *Star Trek* when a supernova threatens to destroy the planet Romulus? Spock arrives too late with a chemical weapon but launches the substance nevertheless. The reaction to this substance creates a black hole that sends Spock and Nero's ships 129 years into the past. This portal through the natural creative order of the universe allows the future and present Mr. Spock to coexist in the same space-time continuum. This imagery of a black hole helps us grasp that the portal is not a reciprocal mechanism. Spock and Nero are unable to return to their time.

The laws of creative order and divine action physics are foundational in understanding how death, grief, and future hope operate within God's will for us. The natural portal to the afterlife is death, wherein our bodies die at the time appointed by our sovereign God. Unlike with the fictional transporter in *Star Trek*, traveling back and forth between the realms of natural science and divine action physics is not possible for a human on their own. Once someone dies, there is no returning to the original human condition.

Divine action physics promises a new body and a new life in eternity, contingent on knowing Jesus Christ as your personal Savior. However, as we will see in later chapters, Christ accomplished this transition with minimal effort as He is supernatural, and He is God. He came back and can move bidirectionally between the realms guided by these two laws of physics. When God decides to interrupt creative order, we see the act of a miracle in our fragile world. How awesome would it be to witness this interaction in present day?

So, what does this all mean? God cares, listens, and intervenes according to His will. This is hard to swallow when we feel horrible or numb after a loss. We look for miracles to take away the loss or pain, but disruption in the law of creative order does not happen because we demand it. If it did, then divine interventions would be considered normal and no longer a signpost to the supernatural work (and healing) of God in our hearts.

Visitation of the Lord on His People

Years ago, a publication called *Brothers in Need* was released, containing a listing of hundreds of Mennonites alongside their addresses and phone numbers. Armed with this information, Mennonites traveling the county would "drop in" on a brother for a visit. There was no expectation for the traveler to pay.

My parents were often irritated by phone calls from folks requesting to visit. We weren't Mennonites and were not listed in the book, but Mennonite relatives would refer other traveling Mennonites to my parents. Many times, they showed up at mealtime, forcing my parents to take them out to eat. Clearly, a good idea had gone wrong.

This is not what the Bible describes as the visitation of the Lord. His unexpected presence brings healing and revitalization, not inconvenience and frustration. The biblical meaning of the word "visit" ranges from "observing" to "being concerned about" or "to care for."

We see in the Old Testament that when God sees people in need, He leans in to provide for them. Key examples include Sarah, Hannah, and Ruth; the Lord remembers them by providing them with children. Once again, God reverses the effects of the natural order, whether it be childbirth, famine, or multiple brushes with death.

Without the visitation of the Lord in our lives, life would be bitter and discouraging. We must hold tight to the promises of God providing for our physical and emotional needs. This means that when God exercises His presence, it is always in the right moment. There are numerous examples: God reverses droughts, drowns Pharoah's cavalry units, and wrestles with Jacob all night long.

We may feel like to Jacob at times. Grief and sadness are emotions we will wrestle with nightly, hoping for relief from mourning our loved ones. This visitation does not mean that God shows up on our front step, visits briefly, and then departs. When God visits upon our hearts, He provides relief, rescue, and deliverance from the emotional whirlwind. When it all suddenly stops, we can hear the wind blow and feel the grass beneath our feet. Everything is peaceful and calm.

God will make this clear to us in His time. We must hold on to the fact that God has prepared supernatural work (divine action physics) once a believer has been ushered through death's door. A new frontier exists, replacing this human life with something much better than what we can presently see, touch, and taste.

If we believe that Christ died and was buried and after three days was raised up, then we must acknowledge that death is not the final frontier. Rather, physical death will usher us into the glorious presence of our Savior and an eternal reunion with our loved ones. We know this because the risen Christ has been there and done that.

Once we acknowledge that divine action physics is the final frontier, our souls begin to reawaken.

I encourage you to step into this movement by undertaking the following:

- Reflect on the love of the Lord in your life. Hold tight to the Psalms for comfort and the reassurance of your value in God's mind. True love casts out all fear, including the fear of death.
- Keep a keen lookout for micromiracles in your daily routines. Small smiles from others and kind words can keep us in step with this movement. It is no accident that God uses others to express His care towards us.
- Believe that divine action physics exists for the ultimate purpose of bringing us joy and peace. He has been preparing this supernatural work just for you. Work through any doubts now so you can step into the next major movement of enjoying a deeper closeness with the Lord.

We never know when God will show up on the front porch of our hearts.

Do not worry about how messy your heart is. He wants to visit with us right where we are.

For more answers to your questions or more information, hover over this QR code and follow the link to our website.

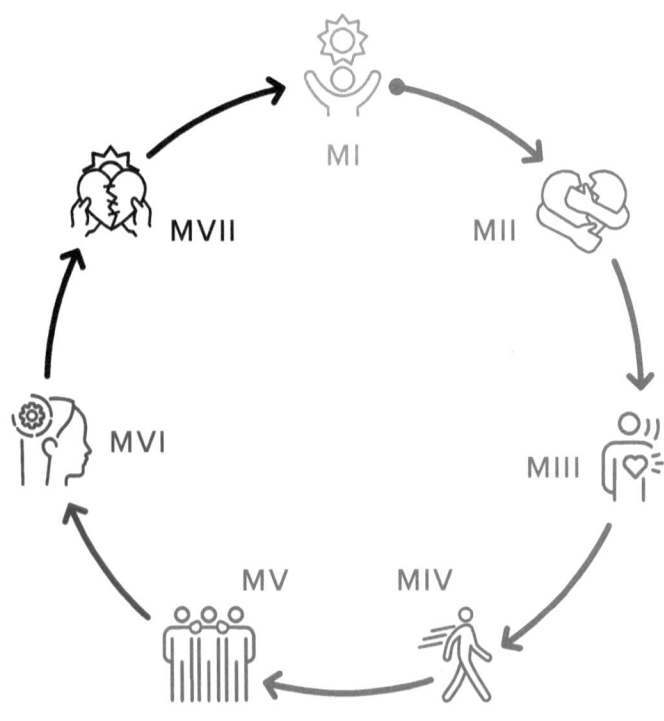

MOVEMENT VII: Achieving a new identity, physical health, emotional health, and spiritual well-being.

MOVEMENT VII

Revitalizing Our Physical and Emotional Health

Enhanced Spiritual Well-Being Identity

Our final destination is revitalizing our identity, physical health, emotional health, and enhanced spiritual well-being.

During my years writing this book, I participated in a life-changing weight-loss program. I was skeptical of the claims, even though they were evidence driven. I have now lost 100 pounds. As I shed the weight, my energy increased, and I became more motivated to exercise. This process was challenging. I did not see significant weight loss right away, but before long, the number on the scale started to decrease consistently.

Within six months, I was feeling great, thinking clearly, more motivated to be active, and had increased mental and emotional stamina.

My walk with God came more into focus as food—my go-to escape—was no longer my way to cope with my stress. The comfort of God moved in my heart during my daily devotions. My true and deeper identity began to emerge, inspiring me to return to the activities I loved, such as hiking, biking, and swimming. More importantly, the comfort of God increased my self-awareness of how

God had gifted me. I came alive!

Losing weight has brought out the features my DNA constructed. I look younger and have the energy and health of an eighteen-year-old. Shedding the grief of who I was allowed me to strengthen who I am. The true nature of God lies in the end result of this revitalization.

Job's ability to revitalize is contingent upon his recalibration of the nature of God and his connection with his loss. The Lord breaks through the silence because Job speaks truth about life, loss, and Himself (Job 42:8).

This is revitalization: developing a more profound joy in the truth of life and how God has the right to give blessings but also take them away without our permission. Both are part of God's promise of resurrection and reunion with our saved loved ones.

Revitalization has another side: the obligation to convey the benefits of looking into the face of Jesus through life's challenges and difficulties to our children and our children's children. Job sees four generations of his children before he passes, and I believe he shares the wonderful workings of God with them.

Anyone want to go riding with me? I have a second bike, and I would love to share the journey with you. Keep pedaling!

CHAPTER 12

The Silver Pocket Knife

"The giving of gifts supports strong love bonds."

One Christmas Day a few years after my dad passed, Mom gave me my dad's jewelry box. There were tie tacks, cuff links, and his silver pocketknife. I took a few items, including the knife. When I arrived home, memories flooded my heart, overwhelming me with emotion. At one point, I could not pick up the knife because the memories of my dad were too acute.

This knife was my dad's favorite, and he was never without it. It was the Swiss pocketknife for gentlemen. My mixed emotions stemmed from a difficult season in my dad's life. Due to the stress of managing two manufacturing plants across town, he was overstretched, and sometimes he went "military grade" on me in response to my childish behaviors. What he did has shaped me into the man I am now, but it was rough back then. I did not help the situation by being a mouthy teenager.

When I touched the pocketknife, those memories overwhelmed me.

My brothers were surprised Mom had given me the jewelry box without involving them. But she had her reasons. They questioned why I had such painful memories connected to my dad's knife.

This artifact was my closest, most intimate connection to my dad after his passing. It was like I was in his presence all over again. He had a rule that I could not touch or take his knife, and simply holding the knife brought back his commanding presence. Because of the high value he placed on the knife, it had become an identity marker.

I had to give it back. I was not ready to enjoy it.

Now, let me explain what an identity marker is and what is not.

First, our sense of identity can be unconsciously swayed by how we think others see us. This can define us in a positive or negative way. As we mature and experience adult situations, our identity becomes fluid, and eventually we delve into who we think we are and how we think the world perceives us.

A marker is a unique quality or characteristic of a person's identity. This can be special ability, skills, attitude, or emotional or cognitive capacities. Some of those core markers last beyond the grave. King David affirms this in Psalm 139, where he writes that God wonderfully formed his inner parts and David's soul has intimate knowledge with Him.

King David's son, Solomon, writes that when our body returns to dust, our soul returns to God who gave it (Ecclesiastes 12:7). How God has formed us in the inner being of our souls is our identity marker.

Now for what our identity marker is not. It is not shaped by our race, gender, nationality, spiritual beliefs, and especially not politics. Each of these can exert some influence on our identity marker, but the core DNA remains the same.

God, who is all-wise, placed us into vessels called bodies in a specific location, as the right race, to glorify Him in all things. This expresses the manifold wisdom of God.

When our loved ones leave, personal items remain like a time capsule of their presence.

For at least ten years, Mom kept Dad's garage stuff and would not give anything away. We could have used them, but Mom would say, "I might need that." By the time she was ready to go through his tools and workbench, all the boys had their own household sets of tools—though we did take some items for ourselves as a connection to Dad and some for our children.

Before Mom was ready to go through the garage stuff, it felt good to see it just how it was on the day he died: the June 1995 calendar still hanging on the workbench, his tools and supplies still organized. Those moments brought back fond memories of his presence in his space. It was comforting.

When you are ready to seek out your loved one's identity markers in your new world, here are some thoughts to consider. If you are unsure of an object, speak up and say, "I might want that, but give me some time to think about it." You can always change your mind to accept it or move on. Unfortunately, many things I was not sure about were passed along to my brothers. Maybe that was for the best.

Choose immediately those personal effects that have strong meaning for you. I loved my parents' clock on the fireplace. I loved seeing the outside thermostat attached to the kitchen window. I also selected a cool, retro, four-in-one yellow-ball-handled screwdriver. I remember the Christmas my dad got it. He thought it was super cool. So did I.

Take a moment to think about those personal items that would be meaningful to you. What brings fond memories of your loved one's loving legacy? You can always find a replica of an item you miss. It does not have to be the exact item they owned.

Do not be bashful about telling your loved ones you are interested in some of their personal effects. They would love to know what interests you and why it is meaningful to you. This can draw both of you together in reminding each other of the personal connections. This also brings them some closure in knowing an item they cherish will be carried on in the family when they are gone. It generates a deep joy.

Encourage your loved one to list all their furnishings and to mark down who would like them. This empowers them in the face of pending death. The giving of gifts supports strong love bonds. You can create new meaning and purpose by celebrating the values and the positive influences that shaped your life.

This is what makes identity markers last in our memories. It is a good thing they are embedded in our souls. God knew what He was doing when He created us now and for the future.

What is your silver pocketknife? I do not regret giving Dad's to one of my brothers. Why? Because he is enjoying it. Someday, I will work through those final remnant thoughts and transform them by buying my own flat silver pocketknife.

CHAPTER 13

The Strawberry Patch Principle

"If we allow those small drops of goodness to soak into our hearts, the patch of grace will cover our ragged edges."

My parents grew up on farms in the Depression, and they learned that a large garden was an excellent way to provide for a large family. We would enjoy potatoes, tomatoes, carrots, lettuce, cucumbers, and strawberries. The strawberries were in a separate patch between my yellow sandbox and the main garden.

This was the patch between pain and pleasure. I was responsible for pulling the weeds in the patch and keeping the strawberries watered. Preparing the patch started in April for June-bearing strawberries. This meant the six-foot-by-six-foot parcel needed to be tilled and picked clean. This was done by a hand rake and on my knees—tricky for a five-year-old.

Planting the strawberry roots required my mom's help to ensure they were spaced properly and the runner plants were not tangled up when placing them in the ground. Caring for the patch meant pulling the large water hose through the grass for about thirty yards from the backdoor of the garage. Again, tough work for a young boy. Watering had to be done early in the day, then weeding around early evening while everyone else was working the main garden. I hated pulling weeds.

Harvesting the patch required patience. All the work had built up to this: plucking the berries gently with my fingers and placing them in a small basket. My mother would clean and dice them into a sweet sauce destined for the refrigerator.

Then, the moment of truth. Making homemade vanilla ice cream, adding Mom's secret gooey chocolate syrup, and finally topping with the strawberries in their sauce made all the pain and toil of the hot June and July melt away on my taste buds. That's when pleasure pinned pain to the mat.

The apostle Paul connects the concept of a germinating seed to burying our bodies in the dirt to be raised into a whole new being through the resurrection of Christ (1 Corinthians 15:20). Our bodies are corruptible, meaning they will degenerate and die. Paul is making the point that the death process brings transformation (1 Corinthians 15:44).

Remember Naomi back in the first chapter of Ruth? She does not see the joy in the process until the very end of her redemption by Boaz. When Ruth and Naomi make their way through Bethlehem, she corrects her friends, telling them her name is no longer "Pleasant" or Naomi, but "Bitter" or Mara (Ruth 1:20).

Naomi continues to say to her friends that she left "full" and the Lord brought her back "empty" (Ruth 1:21). In reality, she left empty in her own broken identity and poor spiritual well-being. What she hasn't experienced is the transformational strawberry patch principle that comes through the process of death. The other side of reality is that she does come back full due to hearing and seeing God provide while in her grief in Moab. She returns in hand with Ruth.

This is God's final movement in bringing a restored sense of our identities, physical health, emotional health, and enhanced spiritual well-being. This movement introduces a new lens of faith that points us towards our resurrection in Christ.

In Israel today, to greet someone or say goodbye, people say, "Shalom." They are literally saying, "May you be full of well-being" or "May health and prosperity be upon you." How do we know if we are in this state of well-being after the loss of a loved one? These three bullets below are characteristics of the final movement of God in our lives. If we can say yes at some level to all three, then we have pivoted into the final movement of revitalization.

- Biblical Identity: I am now comfortable with who I am in the Lord.
- Biblical Worldview: I am now comfortable with making sense of the world and how it functions.
- Biblical Theology: I am comfortable with who God is and how He functions in the world.

How do we keep from drifting out of these movements of God in our lives? Just like with any dance step or practicing the piano, daily moments of reflection on the drops of goodness that come into our days will keep us centered in God. When we are able to look into our strawberry basket, we will see those moments of God's comfort in our lives.

If we allow those small drops of goodness to soak into our hearts, the patch of grace will cover our ragged edges. With God's handiwork, we will emerge into a new tapestry in our hearts, minds, and souls.

I pray that this book somehow helps you feel like Jesus is stitching your ragged edge of emotions into the smooth, silky garment of God's presence.

Are you ready for a bowl of homemade ice cream, gooey chocolate, and delicious, cold, sweet strawberries? Let's taste the goodness of God!

CHAPTER 14

Commencement

"Do something bold!"

I think it is fitting not to have a conclusion for this type of heart work. We never have conclusions but rather new beginnings, like a commencement or graduation.

Consider this moment your certificate of completion in the movements of God. It feels good to accomplish something!

Two Stitches and a Patch is a journey of hope, healing, and health when life-altering events disrupt our lives. I hope you share this book with someone like you. They too need to learn to listen to the whispers of God's love.

You have met my mother, Ruth; my dad, Vernon; my brothers; and Lewis. Each one spoke gently into my heart, opening me up to the healing hand of God during my journey into being a mature man of God.

This healing hand moves us back into being present in the moment (reassociating). We learned to focus on the good memories of our loved ones (reinforcing). It was difficult to express our emotions while not hushing the message (reintegrating). We accepted help out of the deadly pit of regret (reaffirming). We have leaned into supportive relationships (restoring). Life is now becoming meaningful and purposeful (recalibrating). Finally, we experience the peaceful well-being of God's shalom (revitalizing).

I love how King David expresses these seven movements of God in Psalm 30, verses 11 and 12:

> "You turned my lament into dancing;
> You removed my sackcloth and clothed me with gladness, so,
> I can sing to You and not be silent.
> Lord, my God, I will praise You forever."

Thank you for taking this journey with me. Do something you've always wanted to do, like hiking, water-skiing, skydiving, writing that book, calling a friend for coffee, traveling, or picking up a new hobby. I want you to do something bold that expresses this final movement of gladness in your heart.

Call me! I would love to share your joy.

Terry

For more answers to your questions or more information, hover over this QR code and follow the link to our website.

DEDICATION

This book is dedicated to my family, who has supported me during this time of reflecting, processing, and writing memories about Mom and Dad and their profound influence on my life. I am most grateful to my older brothers, Ron, Roger, and Steve, who encouraged me through each stage of writing and remembering a life lived well on Grandview Street.

Thank you to my wife, Becki, for your immeasurable patience and support as I wrote this manuscript.

It is also my desire that our sons, Luke and Matthew, hold tight to the legacy of faith that exists within these pages. I want you to never forget your redheaded, Jesus-loving grandmother and your grandfather, who loved playing whiffle ball in the backyard with you. May you cherish those memories and learn to grieve well when the divine winds of change take me home to Jesus. Lean into the divine work of God in stitching up a new patch for the journey ahead.

Finally, I am dedicating this to my faithful students who had to endure my teaching and mentoring in their undergraduate, graduate, and doctoral classes. This includes those who recently journeyed with me in the exposition of God's Word during our Sunday school class. Your passion for learning and your loving fellowship undergirded the teaching of these important principles. You have been forgiving, understanding, and open to learning the glory of God's Word with me. I am your fellow student of God, as many of us have experienced the divine stitching of God's work in our hearts.

ACKNOWLEDGMENTS

I want to express my deepest appreciation to Robert Lofthouse, my advocate and encourager, who kept me on task when I was frustrated or wanted to stop writing. His encouragement and support turned my thoughts into reality. I am grateful for the hours invested in bringing this book to the finish line. This book would not have been possible without his insight and mentorship.

I also extend my sincere thanks to Bob Goff, who inspired me to discover who I really am and live out that purpose through my writing. Thank you for being Jesus to me when the road was dusty and discouraging. Your words were a cup of cool water for a weary writer. I look forward to being inspired to deliver the next big message from my heart, my friend.

I would be remiss not to mention former professors who taught me the discipline of lifetime learning. Several teachers encouraged me to use my writings to help others by sharing the healing message Jesus laid upon my heart. I am sorry it has taken so long to live out your encouragement, but you saw in me this potential, and now is the time to share.

Special thanks to John Koehler with Koehler Books Publishing for his years of wisdom and direction, including his team of wonderful editors, illustrators, and graphic designers. They have been such a pleasure to work with, knowing that they desire to see my message reach others through their journey of change and transformation.

BIBLIOGRAPHY

Albom, Mitch. *The Five People You Meet in Heaven*. New York, New York: Hyperion Books, 2003.

Bauer, Walter, and Frederick William Danker. *A Greek-English Lexicon of the New Testament and Other Early Christian Literature, 3rd Edition*. Chicago: University of Chicago Press, 2000.

Brown, Francis, S. R. Driver, and Charles A. Briggs, *The Brown-Driver-Briggs Hebrew and English Lexicon*. Peabody, Massachusetts: Hendrickson Academic, 1994.

Fee, Gordon D. *Paul's Letter to the Philippians*. Grand Rapids, Michigan: William B. Errdmans Publishing Company, 1995.

Goff, Bob. *Undistracted: Capturing Your Purpose Rediscover Your Joy*. Nashville, Tennessee: Thomas Nelson Publishing, 2022.

Harris, Murray. *The New International Greek Testament Commentary: The First Epistle to the Corinthians*. Grand Rapids, Michigan: Errdmans Publishing Company, 2005.

Kubler-Ross, Elisabeth. *On Death and Dying: What the Dying Have to Teach Doctors, Nurses, Clergy and Their Own Families (50th Anniversary)*. New York: Scribner Publishing; Reissue edition, 2014.

Mettinger, Tryggve. *In Search of God: The Meaning and Message of the Everlasting Names*. Minneapolis, Minnesota: Fortress Press, 1988.

Pearcey, Nancy. *Total Truth: Liberating Christianity from Its Cultural Captivity*. Wheaton, Illinois: Crossway Books, 2004.

Plantinga, Alvin. *Where the Conflict Really Lies: Science, Religion, & Naturalism*. New York: Oxford University Press, 2011.

Porowski, James, and Paul Carlise. *Strength for the Journey: A Biblical Perspective on Discouragement and Depression*. Nashville, Tennessee: LifeWay Press, 1999.

Prior, Karen Swallow. *On Reading Well: Finding the Good Life through Great Books*. Grand Rapids, Michigan: Brazos Press, 2018.

Savage, Timothy B. *Power through Weakness. Understanding the Christian Ministry in 2 Corinthians*. Cambridge, United Kingdom: Cambridge University Press, 1996.

Saakvitne, Karen W, Sarah Gamble, Laurie Anne Pearlman, and Beth Tabor Lev. *Risking Connection: A Training Curriculum for Working with Survivors of Childhood Abuse*. Brooklandville, Maryland: Sidran Institute Press, 1999.

Thiselton, Anthony C. *The New International Greek Testament Commentary: The First Epistle to the Corinthians*. Grand Rapids, Michigan: Errdmans Publishing Company, 2000.

www.ingramcontent.com/pod-product-compliance
Lightning Source LLC
LaVergne TN
LVHW041613070526
838199LV00052B/3128